A MASTERCLASS in NEEDLE FELTING DOGS

Methods and techniques to take your needle felting to the next level

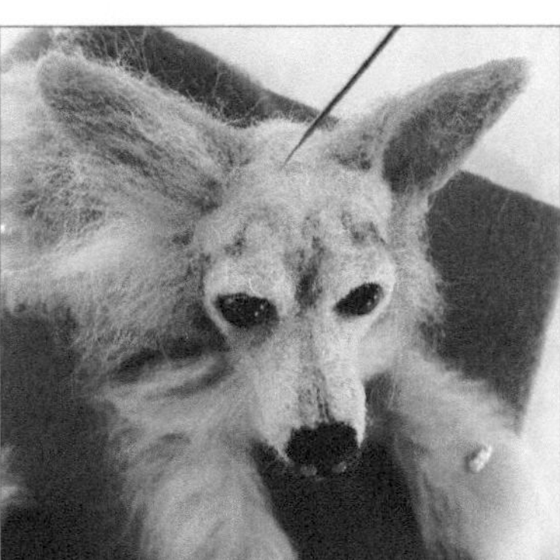

The Hubble & Hattie imprint offers a range of books that cover all things animal, promoting compassion, understanding and respect between all animals (including humans!)

Also in this series

A Masterclass in Needle Felting Wildlife (Thompson)

A Masterclass in Needle Felting Endangered Species (Thompson)

Some more great books from Hubble & Hattie!

Animal Grief: How animals mourn (Alderton)

Cat and Dog Health, The Complete Book of (Hansen)

Complete Dog Massage Manual, The – Gentle Dog Care (Robertson)

Confessions of a veterinary nurse: paws, claws and puppy dog tails (Ison)

Detector Dog – A Talking Dogs Scentwork Manual (Mackinnon)

Dinner with Rover: delicious, nutritious meals for you and your dog to share (Paton-Ayre)

Dog Cookies: healthy, allergen-free treat recipes for your dog (Schöps)

Emergency First Aid for dogs: at home and away Revised Edition (Bucksch)

Fun and Games for Cats (Seidl)

Gods, ghosts, and black dogs – the fascinating folklore and mythology of dogs (Coren)

Tale of two horses – a passion for free will teaching (Gregory)

Unleashing the healing power of animals: True stories about therapy animals – and what they do for us (Preece-Kelly)

Wildlife Garden (Kopp)

Wildlife photography from the edge (Williams)

www.hubbleandhattie.com

First published September 2020 by by Hubble & Hattie, an imprint of David and Charles Limited. Tel +44 (0)1305 260068 / e-mail info@hubbleandhattie.com/web www.hubbleandhattie.com. Reprinted 2020, 2021, 2022 and 2024.
ISBN: 978-1-787113-83-1
 British Library Cataloguing in Publication Data – A catalogue record for this book is available from the British Library. Design and DTP by Veloce. Printed and bound by TJ Books Ltd, Padstow, Cornwall.

CONTENTS

DEDICATION & ACKNOWLEDGEMENTS

I dedicate this book to my late grandmother, Mrs Vera E Carpenter – 'Mum.' Without her love and encouragement during my formative years of all things art and dogs, my path through life would have been different. I know she would be very proud of my achievement.

A huge thank you to my loving husband, Alan, who has been right beside me through my illness, and supporting me when writing this book. He's one in a million.

Thank you to Jude, Joe, and Kevin at Hubble & Hattie, who have worked so hard in getting my book into print, and also to the rest of the team there working behind the scenes.

PREFACE

I was raised by my grandmother, who I called mum. She ran a large business – all-things dog in the Bedfordshire countryside – and we lived in a 450 year old timber-framed, mud and daub thatched cottage. Mum was a very well-respected dog trainer, who ran her own competitive dog training club, and set some well-known professional dog trainers on their paths to specialised work. She bred Irish Wolfhounds, and we would compete annually at many championship and exemption shows throughout the year, always culminating with an entry or two at Crufts Dog Show, and also ran boarding kennels and trained dogs for security.

My life was very dog orientated but, being very musical and artistic as a child, I was encouraged by family and an excellent private education to indulge in art and music, and it was my love of art that allowed my creativity to grow.

Whilst I've had varied employment – security dog trainer, dog warden, laboratory technician, courier, private secretary, HGV driver, to name a few (and I also read Arabic at Leeds University) – my love of art was never far away, and I continued to sketch, paint and model animals.

Although I had already backpacked to many countries, my life really changed when I met my husband, Alan, and we decided to move into a converted van, initially, and later a truck, and do some serious independent travelling. Our first big road trip was overland to Kathmandu and back, through 18 countries; 22,366 miles in 12 months. We lived for 13 years on the road, working the summer months in the UK and travelling during the winter months around Europe, Asia and North Africa. We could have continued living this way of life, but something beckoned us to settle down and the timing couldn't have been better. I had been suffering for many years with what were to become very serious bladder/kidney plumbing issues, which became more frequent after we settled in one place, causing a number of serious sepsis infections that almost claimed my life. The situation culminated nine years later in a urostomy, which was a positive move, health-wise.

Whilst recovering from the sepsis episodes I needed something 'arty' to occupy my mind and hands, and I stumbled across needle felting by a famous Japanese artist, Kirino Mirii, who developed the art in the early 2000s in Japan, progressing to become a world class needle felter. I was very fortunate to meet Kirino Mirii in 2017 when she was part of a Japanese art exhibition in London, and was shocked to discover that she knew of me and my work!

At the time I started needle felting there were no books or videos showing how it was done, so I am rather proud of the fact that I am completely self-taught. I bought my first needles from Felt Alive in America, and bargained with a local sheep shearer for a couple of fleeces in return for some homemade marmalade and some of our eggs. I had to find out how to wash and card (brush the wool and make it fluffy) the fleece, and this gave me a good start.

With lots of practice, many disasters and growing interest from those around me, I began to develop my own style and techniques. The art of needle felting was immensely helpful during my health problems as it kept me focused, and gave me something productive to do. As I improved, more people wanted to buy my work, and I actually began selling my creations on eBay, with my first dog, a pug mix, going for £3.33. Once I broke the £100 barrier I set up my own Facebook page, website and other social media sites.

Over the years I have been needle felting – ever willing to push boundaries and make mistakes – I have developed techniques that are not found anywhere else. For example, my method of making realistic eyes, discovered by mistake, has transformed my sculptures, and given them taxidermic eyes in miniature. Discovery of other art mediums that one wouldn't consider mixing with wool have also made a huge difference to the finished sculptures. I shall continue to experiment, make mistakes, and develop more techniques with what is a totally addictive art form.

I'd like to introduce my little helper, at this point, my tabby cat, Monkey (who also answers to Smonks and Punky Monkey). She loves to keep me company whilst I felt, and is sometimes very helpful, telling me to take a rest, or that she'd like to pose with some newly-created sculptures.

She sometimes tries felting herself: here, she spent ages fashioning this cloud, then promptly fell asleep on it ...

I hope that this book will help you on your journey of discovering and then improving your needle felting: whilst it might concentrate on breeds of dog, the techniques shown here should prove useful for any other needle felting subject you might wish to specialise in.

Happy felting!

INTRODUCTION

This book's readership will be those who can confidently use a range of felting needles to felt core wool into any shape or form, and who want to move onto the next step of learning more detailed techniques and methods for creating more realistic needle felted dogs. I recommend that you read through each chapter fully before beginning work on the sculpture.

Although the book showcases four breeds of dog, the techniques and methods used to create these can be transferred to many other animals, and is therefore useful knowledge for any needle felter to have.

Explaining the detailed shaping of these dogs isn't covered, as it is assumed that readers will be able to create the necessary shaping by studying photos of each breed, allowing individual interpretation of each breed and developing a unique style. It does, however, cover the following –

- creating an armature
- initial covering and bulking (adding volume) of core wool
- how to create different poses
- three methods of creating noses
- two methods of creating eyes (one not covered anywhere else)
- how to prepare Merino tops for long coat attachment
- two different methods of attaching Merino tops to create the effect of a long coat
- how to texture the long coat
- how to blend Merino colours to achieve many more shades and hues
- how to add extra finishing colours
- two different methods of creating nails for paws
- how to create accessories: a bowl of food, a biscuit bone, and a collar & lead

With good basic needle felting knowledge and a little knowledge of dog shapes, all of the projects in this book can be created.

Like any other art form, needle felting requires practice and more practice. I am still learning every day, and each sculpture I create teaches me something new!

The best advice I can give is never be afraid to make mistakes. All of my mistakes have taught me so many things, even if it's what not to repeat. Fear of failure can cause a serious artistic block, and if I had a fear of failing, I would not be sharing this information.

So please don't be afraid to try in case it doesn't go to plan. Go with the flow and see where it takes you ...

GETTING STARTED: TOOLS & EQUIPMENT

Felting tools

Needle felting is a relatively inexpensive craft, and there is a wide range of tools and wool to choose from, depending on what you want to create. As this versatile craft increases in popularity, so too will the types of tools, materials and creations. It's possible to get started with a basic set of six needles (usually described as fine, medium and coarse), a felting pad, an awl and scissors; all for a couple of pounds on eBay. Add to this a decent beginner's variety pack of core wool, and you can begin needle felting.

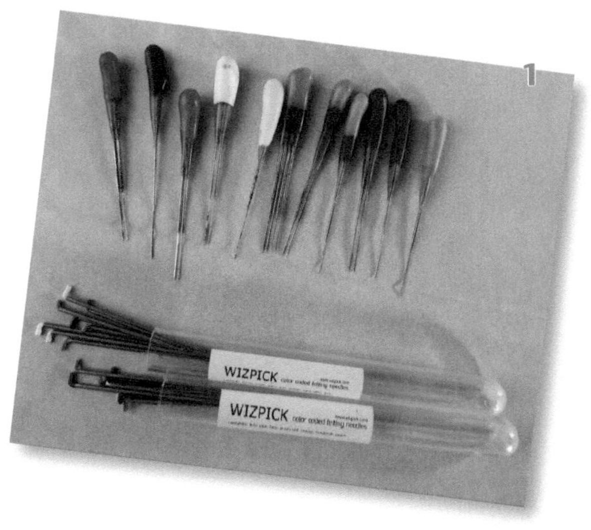

Needles

1

The Clover multi-tool is a sprung 5-needle holder used for creating flat, thin felt, or adding embellishment to a flat surface. Found on eBay, I particularly use this tool for creating ears on a felting brush. There is a cheaper version which has seven needles and is equally effective.

A firm favourite of mine is the 3-in-line holder, in which I place dark green HeidiFeathers needles (www.heidifeathers.com) that are excellent for fast shaping and bedding down, and can be purchased from Adelaide Walker (www.adelaidewalker.co.uk). Various double needles are a speciality of Felt Alive (www.feltalive.com), an American company that makes a very useful set of needles with colour-coded rubber handles that are easy to hold and use, and easily distinguished at a distance.

One of my most used Felt Alive double needles is the green reverse. Felt Alive also makes quad needles, which make very effective combs for texturing long fur. Wiz Pick (www.wizpick.com) does an excellent range of specialised needles, and have needles found nowhere else. My most used of this range are the Aqua, Red, and White.

Handles

If you like to hold something more substantial, you can buy a variety of needle holders, which can hold single needles or a number of needles (needles can be changed as needed).

Awl and pins
2

I couldn't needle felt without an awl, which can be used for fitting and painting eyes, pulling out shape, lifting ears from a felting brush and generally poking about. Found on eBay, included in a starter felting tool kit for a couple of pounds. Pins, the round-headed types, are useful for keeping nostrils open whilst you work on them, and the large, flat-headed type is useful for securing a sculpture onto a felting foam whilst you work on it.

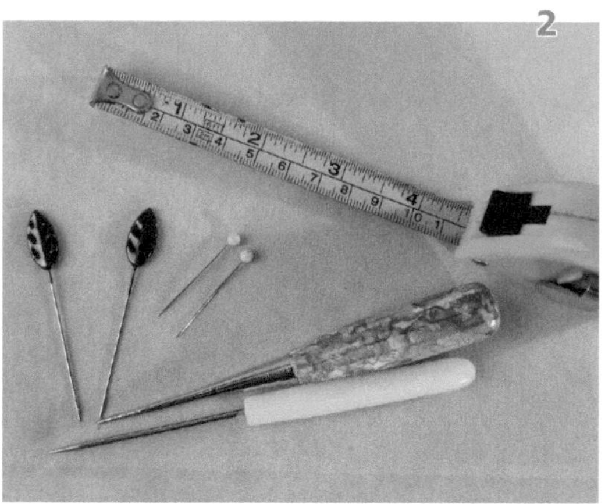
2

Pliers, wire cutters and tape measure
3

You will need at least one pair of ridged needle pliers. Don't buy the smooth-surfaced ones, as the ridged working surface helps grip the wire and hold it in place as you use the pliers. You may sometimes need two pairs: when making accessories, for example.

Any size of wire cutters will do the job, though ensure they are of reasonable quality so that they last. Readily available in DIY and pound shops.

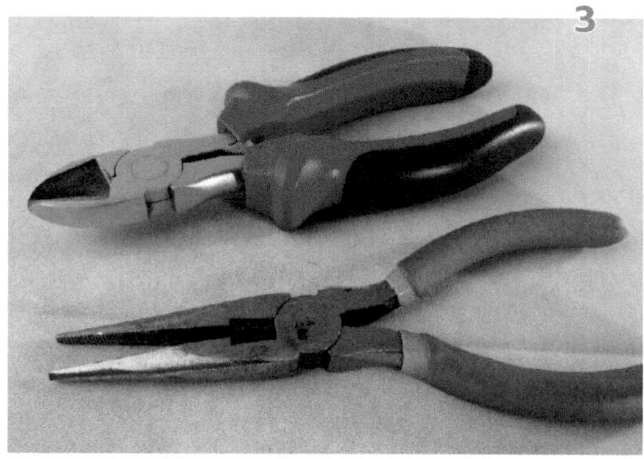
3

Tape measure/ruler

For measuring armature and proportions. Easily found in many High Street shops or online.

Scissors
4

I use a pair of Westcott 4 inch scissors, which are small, pointed and very sharp! With daily use for trimming coats, they last two years, on average. I also have a couple of pairs of small embroidery scissors, which are useful for those more difficult to reach parts as they have a finer and smaller point. A large pair of Westcott scissors are useful for cutting lengths of wool tops, which helps lengthen life expectancy of smaller trimming scissors. Bought on Amazon.

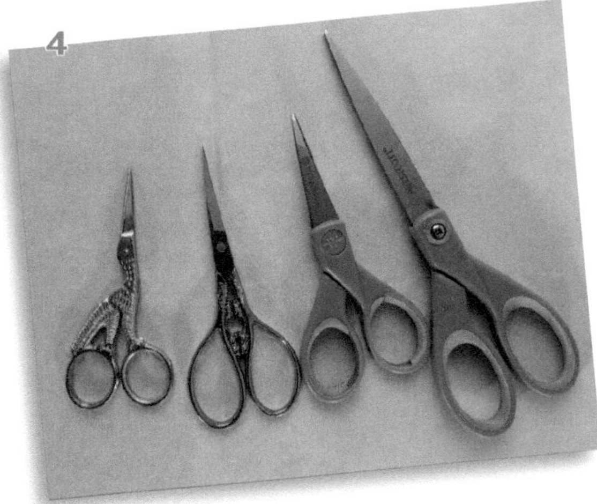
4

Felting foam pads

This is used as a multi-functional surface: as somewhere on which to work; to secure sculptures as you work on them, and to safely hold needles as you work and switch between them. Readily available online.

Wire
5

I mostly use plastic-coated garden wire of around 1.2mm gauge for the armatures, as I find the plastic coating much kinder on both needles and fingers. I also have a range of thinner, non-plastic-coated wires, and a heavier duty plastic-coated one of 1.7mm for animals with longer legs who need more support: horses, for example. The thinner, non-plastic-coated wires I use to fashion buckles for collars and leads, or support FIMO (a brand of polymer clay: see page 10) clay jaws. Wire of all description can be purchased from eBay or Amazon.

Pan Pastels and soft pastels
6

These are a brand of soft pastel that can be used like paint and applied with a brush. Whilst expensive, they will last forever as they have good coverage and a strong pigment. The set used with these projects is the Drawing Set, a ten-colour selection of natural browns, greys and whites, including a black. There are 92 colours in the Pan Pastel range. I also purchased extra colours Burnt Sienna Shade and Orange Shade: all bought on Amazon.

A good set of soft pastels will be useful, too, as these can be used as they come, or else scraped with a knife to make a powder. Available in pound shops.

6

A range of small paint brushes
7

Ideally, from 1cm rough and soft brushes to apply glues, through to very fine and pointed which are perfect for applying the Pan Pastels (readily available in pound shops in the nail art sections).

5

7

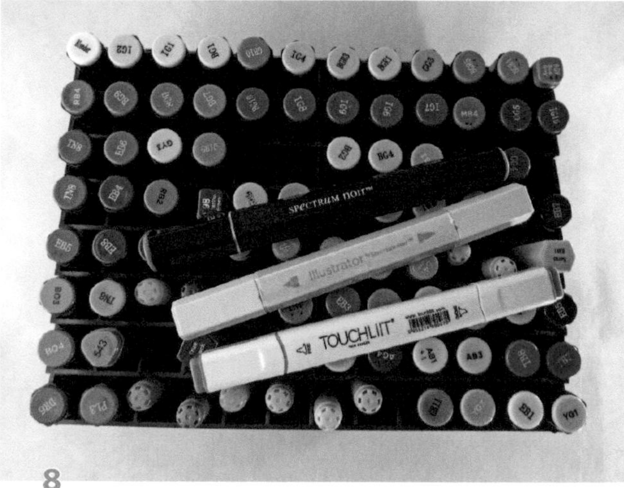

8

Alcohol pens

8

There are a few makes on the market, but most of my marker pens are Spectrum Noir (www.spectrumnoir.com), but I also use Touch Liit and Script Twin Markers, all easily sourced online. These are essential for making eyes, and for colouring and shading wool on the finished sculpture. You can purchase these individually or in packs of similar hues. I mainly use browns, greys, and black, plus a blender. The important point is that they must be alcohol-based and not water-based. Purchased from eBay. (Note: the Chameleon brand pens are water-based, and spoil when used with water-based sealer.)

Glossy Accents™

9

A clear, water-based sealant that adds a three-dimensional, glass-like finish to eyes. There are other makes, but ensure they are water-based so that the sealant can be safely used over the alcohol pens without making the colours run. Readily available in card-making shops and online, and often referred to as Diamond Glaze.

9

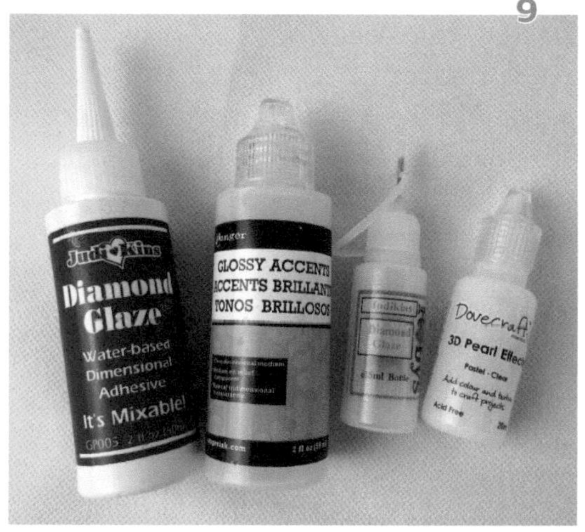

Polymer clay

10

A versatile clay that is cured by baking in a conventional home oven (or a small,

10

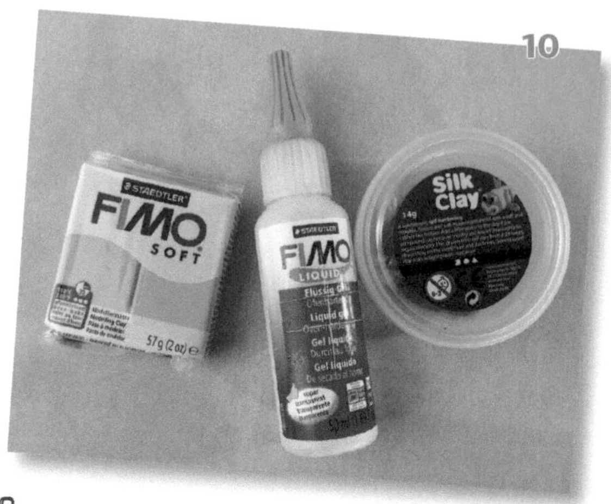

cheaper-to-heat camping oven, but NOT a microwave). This clay can be used to make all manner of accessories, from nails to mouth parts, to dog biscuits. It comes in a huge range of colours that can be easily mixed or coloured with pastels, or painted.

The beauty of polymer clay is that you can bake it many times, each time adding to the item. There are a few makes, and the best known is FIMO. You will also need some liquid FIMO, which is used like a glue to bond additional elements if you bake more than once. Polymer clay is cured by baking in an oven at around 130°C (266°F) for 30 minutes, but the very small amounts used for these projects need a few minutes only. Available on eBay and Amazon.

Silk Clay®

A quick air-drying clay that comes in a range of colours, and begins to set in about ten minutes; sooner if the item is very small. The beauty of Silk Clay is that you can sculpt on the wool sculpture without having to take it off and bake it; possibly deforming it in the process. It doesn't set as hard as polymer clay, but has a softer touch to it. Found on eBay.

Acrylic paint
11

Use a basic set of colours to help colour your baked polymer clay and add fine details to your sculpture. Available on eBay, Amazon and pound shops.

11

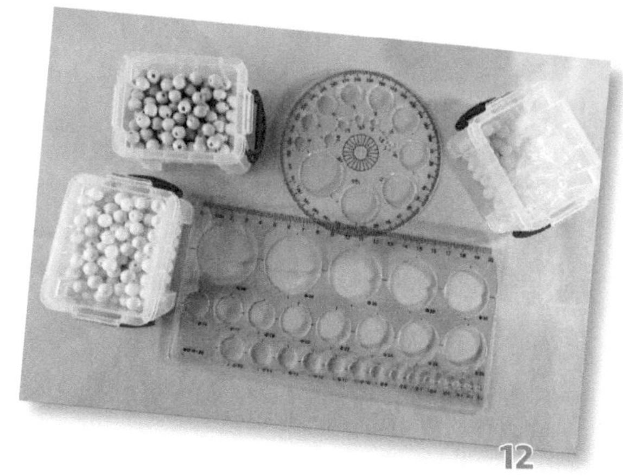
12

Acrylic beads and circle templates
12

You will need various sizes of beads, with 6mm (0.23in) to 12mm (0.47in) the most popular range in this book. Off-white or ivory are the best colours, and can be coloured with alcohol pens. These beads are very easy to colour and fit, and you have no need to worry about the hole through the bead showing, as only a third of a dog's eye is visible when in place with the rest concealed in the eye socket. Unfortunately, beads are available in even sizes only.

To prevent beads being scratched when creating an eye socket, a set of working 'spacer beads' will be required. These can be any colour as they are used only to create the perfect space for the actual eye beads until you are ready to fit these. When the eye surround is completed, simply swap the spacer beads for the finished eyes. Readily available on eBay.

Circle templates are essential for colouring the beads to make the eyes. The template contains the application of colour in a perfect circle on the beads, and ensures they are both the same size: a feat impossible to achieve freehand. You will need a template that includes a range of circles from 3mm (0.11in) through to 11mm (0.43in). For ease of use, I cut this range from the template as they can be rather bulky to handle, and you won't need the other sizes for these projects. Available on eBay.

Leather lace/strips, mini rivets, hole punch, hammer, mini buckles, etc
13

Flat leather lace comes ready-cut in many colours; my most used size is 5mm (1.19in) wide and 1mm (0.03in) thick (any thicker and it becomes very difficult to hole punch and rivet). Perfect for collars and leads. Mini rivets are used for securing the leather of collars and leads, and you'll also need a hole punch, hammer, and a rivet punch set. All of the above are available on eBay.

Mini buckles/rings and chains can be found online from doll accessory shops, and jewellery-finding listings. The chains make good dog collars and the rings finish them off. Buckles are used on the collars and are available on eBay, Amazon, and Etsy. If you like you can add mini charms to your dog collars (usually described as Tibetan Charms), and thin wire can be used to fashion buckles and loops.

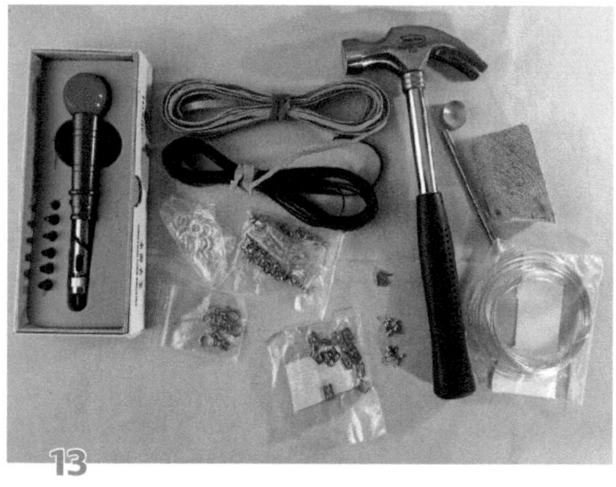
13

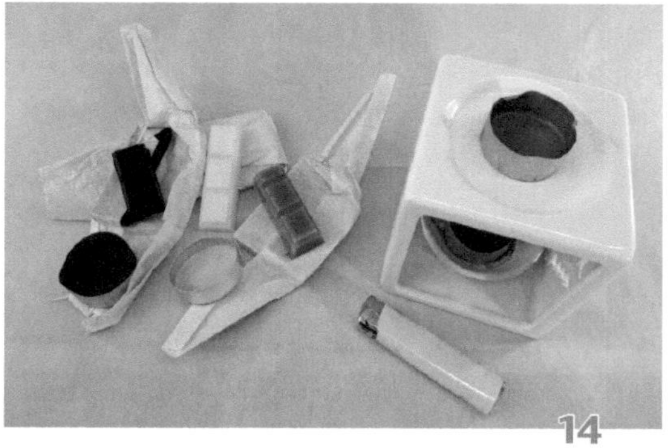
14

Felting wax and ceramic tea-light burner
14

Felting wax is a special blend of wax that melts at low temperature, and can be applied to a felted surface to give a smooth finish that could resemble skin, a nose, etc. To create a harder surface for the wax application, first brush the felted surface with PVA glue and let it dry: this helps prevent the wax from leeching into the wool. Felting wax can be purchased ready coloured, or you can colour it yourself when set with ink or the alcohol pens. Available on Etsy, and from a number of needle felting companies, such as Mum's Makery and The Makerss in the UK, and Sarafina Fibre Art in the US.

A ceramic tea-light oil burner is an essential piece of kit with which to melt the felting wax. The wax can be contained in a spent tea-light candle holder, and placed on the ceramic dish, so that it is melted by the candle below. This keeps the ceramic dish free from wax and the need to clean it before using a different colour. You can also use an electric wax heater, but will still need a flame to heat the metal moulding tools in order to remould your felting wax. Available in pound shops and on eBay.

Modelling tools
15

A range of tools exist – ball tools, flat

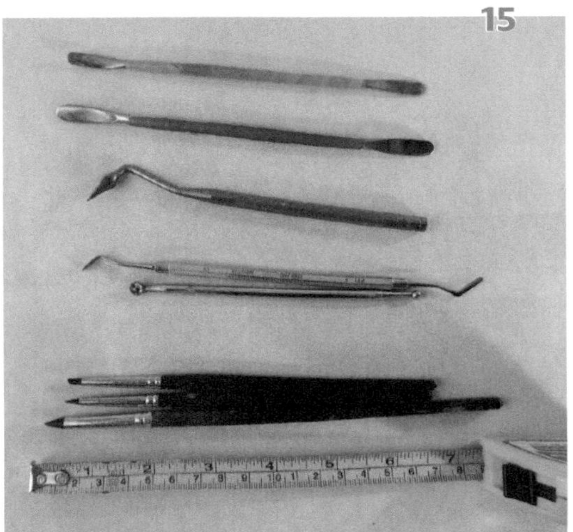
15

tools, etc of different sizes – for moulding polymer clay. Dentistry tools are useful, too, especially when re-moulding the felting wax, as it's possible to heat the end of the tool and easily re-work the wax. You will also need some small, rubber-tipped sculpting for detail work with the silk clay on the eyes. Available on eBay and Amazon as clay modelling or cake decorating tools.

Cabochons, stalks, and downloadable, printable eyes
16

These are half-sphere lenses used in jewellery making. Clear, eye-size examples can be used to make realistic eyes, by sticking them over painted eyes, or printed eyes on glossy photographic paper. They come in various thicknesses, but the lower domed cabochons are better for dogs.

Once the eye colouring is glued in place, you can also glue a stalk onto the back to aid stability and when fitting them into the head. Without the stalk, they are very tricky to fit and secure in place, whilst ensuring they both look in the right direction. Available on eBay.

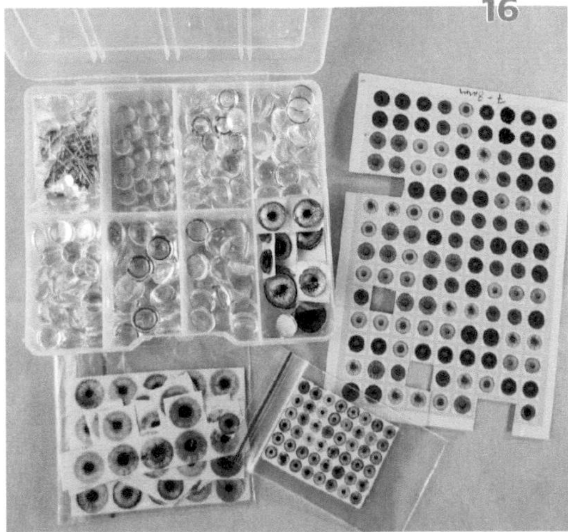
16

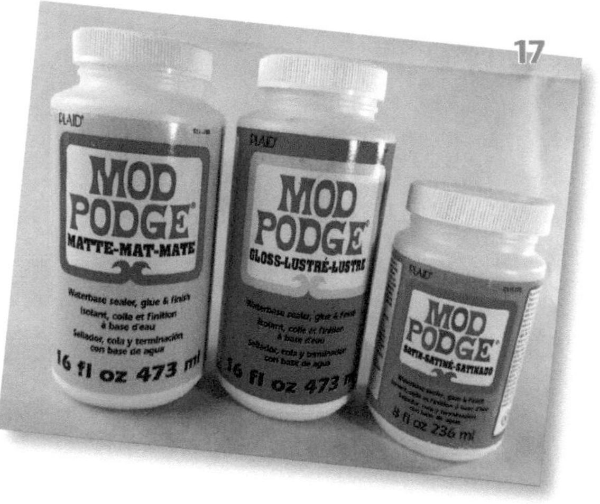

17

Mod Podge®
17

A wonderful range of sealant/glues, that can be used for a variety of jobs, from simply gluing to texturing fur, stiffening the insides of ears to make them retain a certain position, and finishing off glossy mouth parts, noses and nails. I regularly use, matt, silk and gloss versions. Available on eBay and Amazon or in craft stores.

(Many of the items I've listed can be found in good craft stores if you are lucky enough to live near one.)

Wool
18, 19

A quick note about the wool used for these

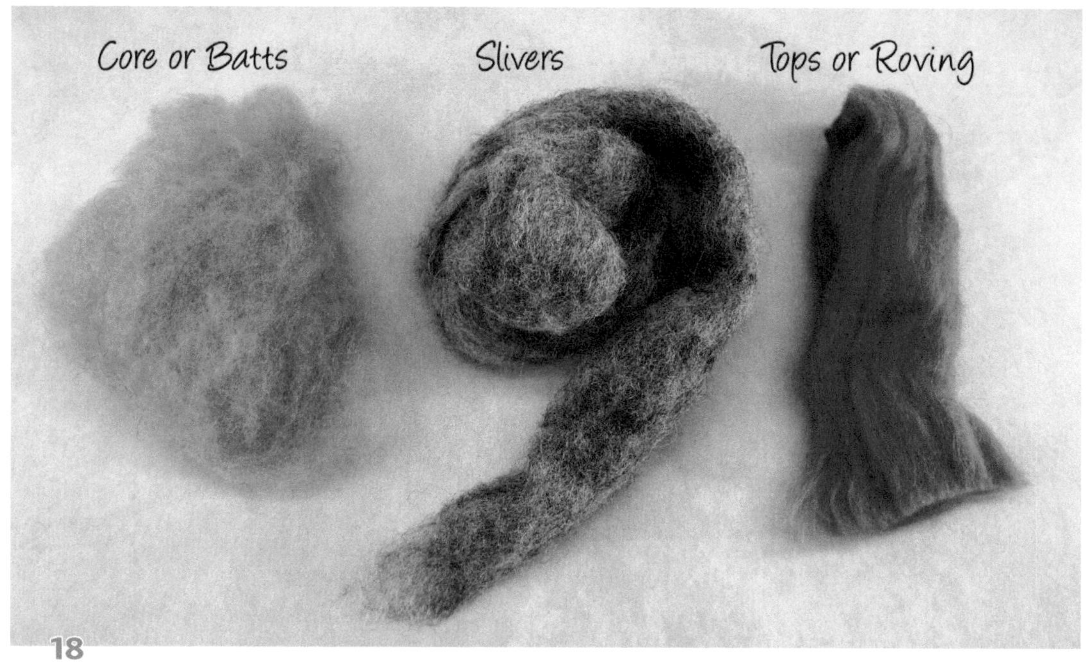

18

projects. There are essentially two types of industrial processed wool, the first of which is core wool.

Sometimes called batts, this is wool that has been washed and carded, resulting in a fluffy mass comprising naturally curly fibres that have become entangled; it is very easy to felt and create shapes with this.

Core wool can also come in slivers, which

19

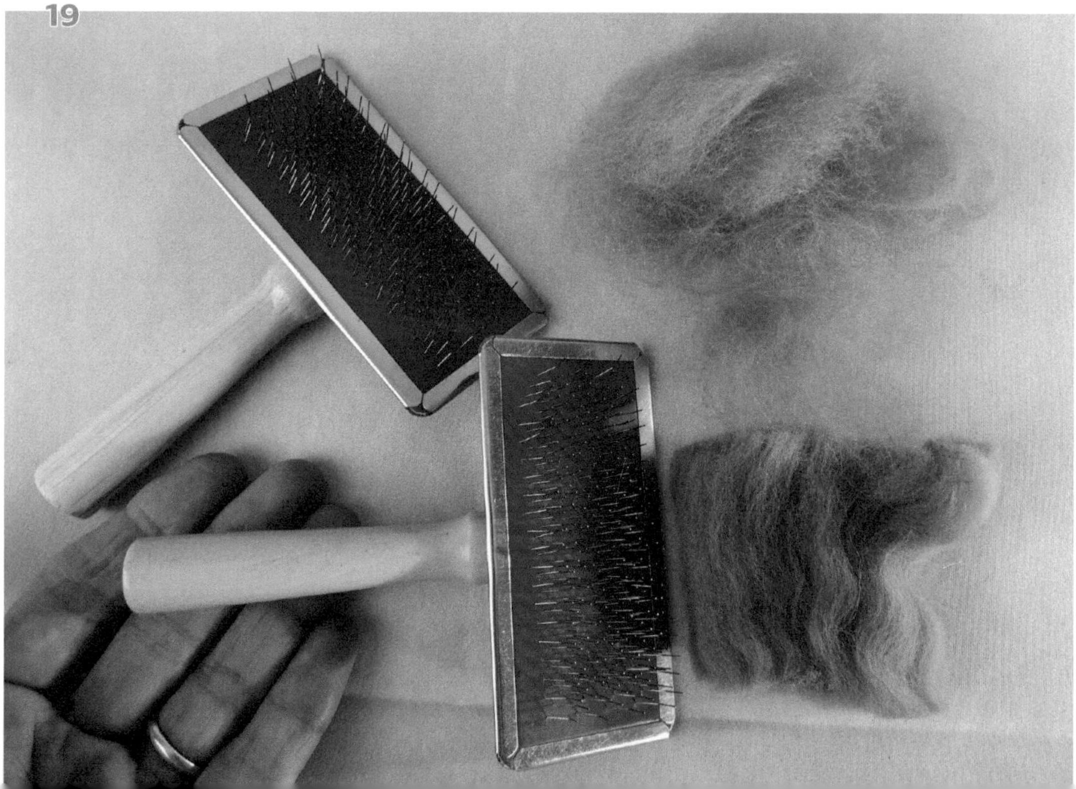

is a long length of processed wool coiled into a ball, and is ideal for wrapping.

All of the projects in this book start with core wool.

Tops (sometimes called roving) is core wool that has been put through another process where it is, in effect, combed and stretched to make the fibres long and straight, and aligned with each other. It is usually sold in a continuous thick length of wool around 2 or 3cm thick, and looks a bit like hair. By far the largest selection of tops colours is in the Merino range, but tops can come from other sheep breeds, too. The Yorkshire Terrier in this book has a coat of Merino tops.

To process the Merino tops a pair of small carders – flat, metal-toothed brushes – are required.

Purpose-made carders are available to buy, or dog brushes of a similar shape make good alternatives. Carders brush, separate and 'fluff' the Merino wool, ready for use on a sculpture, and are essential for blending Merino wool colours. Those shown in the picture are the smallest size, available from The Makerss.

General points

This book assumes that you, dear reader, have good basic knowledge of needle felting; how to use a felting needle and how to add wool to create and maintain shaping, and that you can interpret where form needs to be added. Describing how to make a very complicated, three-dimensional shape, such as a dog's head, would sound very clumsy, so the interpretation of shaping is encouraged and left to the sculptor, where he or she can use their own style.

Throughout the book are tips and tricks to help overcome common issues you may encounter, as well as advise short cuts. You might be surprised, for example, how many felters have never thought of cutting their sculpture, yet a few simple cuts, in the right place, can save many hours of frustration.

Invest in a good range of needles from different manufacturers, and keep trying out different ones as you work. You will soon discover your favourites. What suits one felter, won't suit another, even though they might be doing the same task. Remember also that you can experiment with your multi-holders, by fitting different grade needles.

Last of all, needle felting should be a very relaxing art form. If you are breaking needles, then you are most probably too tense. Relax and keep your touch light and gentle so that you can 'feel' where you are going and what you are creating. There is no need to be heavy-handed or to stab very quickly. If you are using the optimum grade needle for the task in hand, you will find that you can achieve excellent results, felting slowly with purpose.

Let's get going!

THE CHIHUAHUA

The first dog in the book focuses on the initial making of an armature; first coverage of wool, and making eyes and nails, which will not be repeated in such detail in other chapters, as the method is essentially the same for all dogs; only the colours differ. Subsequent chapters will not repeat how to form the armature, or the first covering of wool, or how to colour eyes unless they are a different colour. Only wire lengths and armature plan, eye size and colours used will be given.

Creating this Chihuahua will showcase a standing position, reverse blending felting, making realistic eyes, paws and nails, and some detailing techniques.

Chihuahuas are quite long-bodied with a thick trunk, neck, and large head, but with very thin legs. The front legs are wider set than the hindlegs, and the eyes are large for the size of the dog. Long nails are also a feature of this breed as they tend not to get a lot of exercise!

YOU WILL NEED

Materials

- Wire (16 gauge) and preferably plastic-coated
- Core (natural), 100g (3.9oz)
- Core (light tan), 40g (1.58oz) (The Felt Box No 19)
- Tops (mid-grey), 10g (0.39oz) (World of Wool Merino Tops Pewter)
- Tops (black), 10g (0.39oz) (World of Wool Merino Tops Raven)
- Tops (tan), 10g (0.39oz) (World of Wool Merino Tops Antique)

- Tops (fawn), 10g (0.39oz) (Wingham Wool Merino Tops Fawn)
- 2 x 12mm (0.47in) spacer beads
- 2 x 12mm (0.47in) x2 Ivory/off-white beads for the eyes
- Silk Clay, dark brown (small amount from small container)
- Diamond Glaze or Glossy Accents sealant (either will work)
- UPV clear drying craft glue
- Felting wax, black ,for the nose
- Fine light brown fishing line for the whiskers

Tools

- Wire cutters
- Pliers
- Tape measure/ruler
- Awl
- Scissors, small pointed
- Rubber-tipped sculpting tools (small size)
- Metal clay-dentist tools
- Very fine, 1mm (0.03in) paintbrush (nail art-type brushes are perfect)
- Spectrum Noir pens: GB9, TN7, RB3, EB6, BG6, Black and Blender
- Pan Pastels: various browns, greys, whites and black from the Drawing Set
- A pink/purple pastel for the inside of the ears
- 8mm (0.31in) circle template
- Six large-headed pins
- Two small round-headed pins
- Sandpaper or nail file
- A couple of wire carders. Small wire dog brushes will do the same job
- Kitchen roll; small glass of water
- Carpet needle (curved needle)

METHOD

Step 1

1

Measure out the wire in lengths of 1 x 44cm (17.32in) and 2 x 42cm (16.53in). You will need to trim these once the armature has been formed, but always better to allow extra wire than too little.

The longest length of wire will create the tail, back, neck and head. Starting with the tail, bend to proportions shown in image 1,; armature plan image 4) up the tail, along the back, up the neck and finally the head. The other two lengths are bent in half, and will make the back and front legs.

1

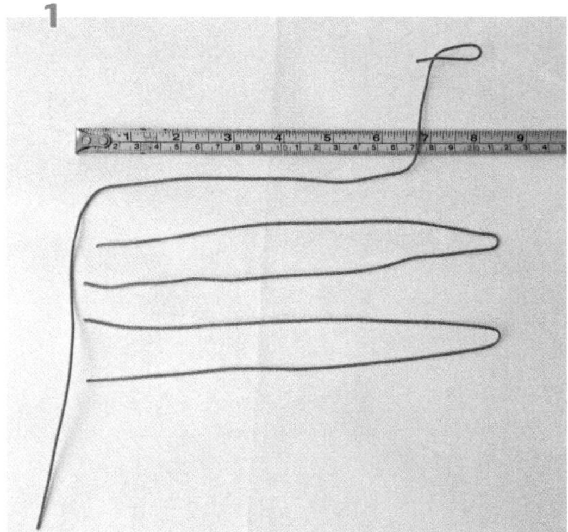

Step 2

2, 3

To attach the legs, loop one of the folded in half pieces of wire over the shoulder area. Firmly holding the body and one leg with one hand, use your other to tightly wrap the other leg around the body, as tightly as you can. Do the same for the back legs, which are to be attached at the hips, or just in front of where the tail starts. You should now be left with a basic armature as shown.

Step 3

4

Bend both sets of legs into shape following the measurements shown, starting at the body and working down to the paw. Bending both legs at the same time will help make them equal.

2

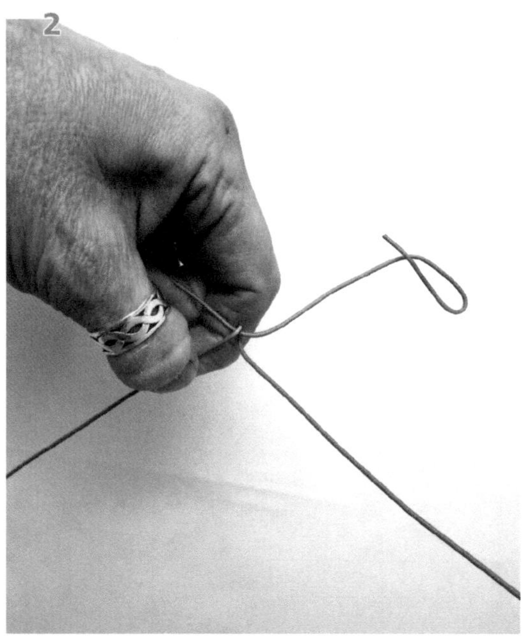

3

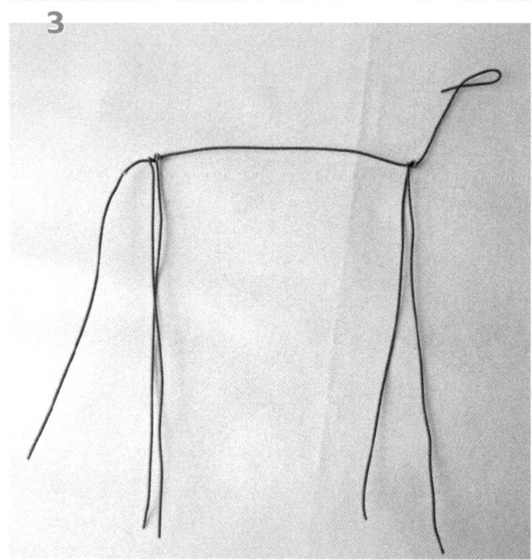

4

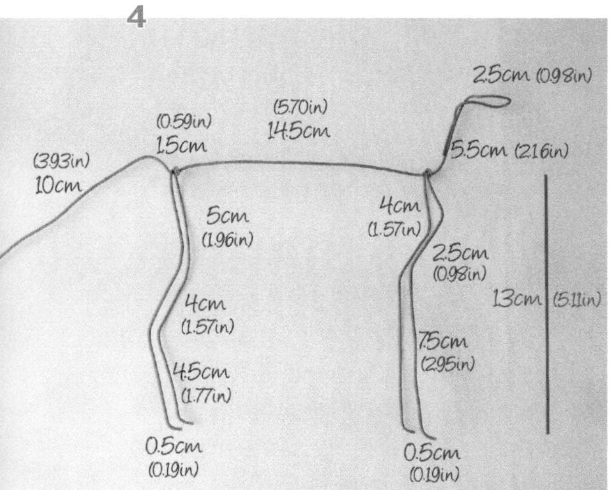

Step 4

5

Once you're happy with your bending, and they are equal and accurate (check and double-check), trim away any excess wire on the paw, making sure you retain 0.5cm (0.19in) for each paw.

Step 5

6

Now arrange the armature so that it can stand square and unaided. This might take a bit of fiddling, but it is a very important step. Part the legs at the body and make the front legs slightly wider apart than the back legs. Once formed, the armature should stand 13cm (5.11in) high at the shoulders, and the head should reach 19cm (7.48in). These measurements will help you achieve the correct angle of bends in the legs.

TIP

It is very important that as you work on your armature you don't bend or squash its form, as this will lead to one leg being longer than the other, or some other deformity. Check that it can stand square and unaided every now and then

Step 6

7-9

To give your armature an initial covering of wool – which will provide the base and anchor for all the other wool – take a roughly 25cm (9.84in) length of white core, 7cm (2.75in) wide in thickness, and start by tightly wrapping around the bottom of the neck, holding the first part of the wrapping secure as you continue to wrap around the bottom of the neck, under the chest; back around the neck. At this point, if you have wrapped tightly enough, you should be able to let go of the beginning.

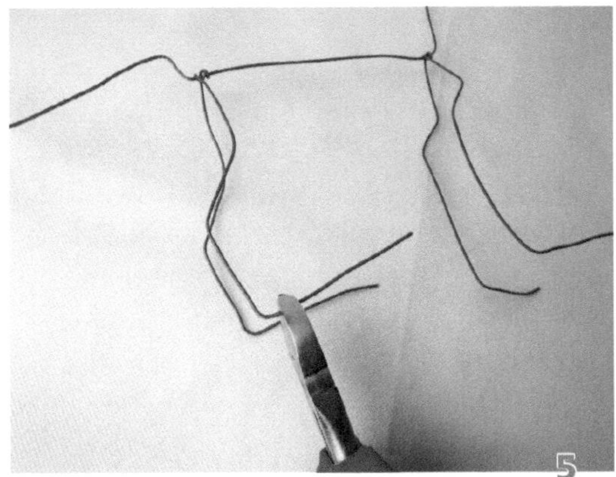
5

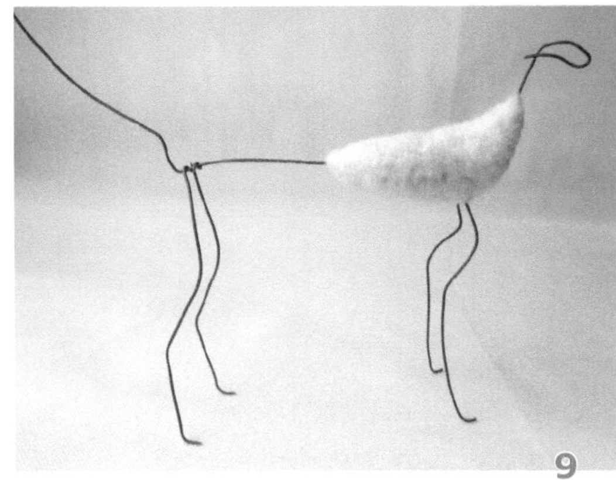
9

6

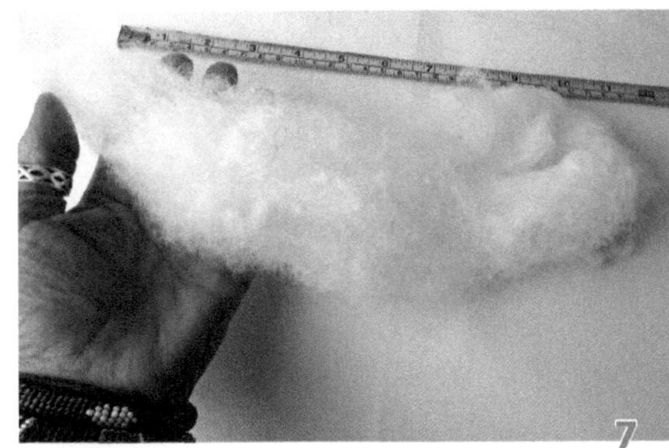
7

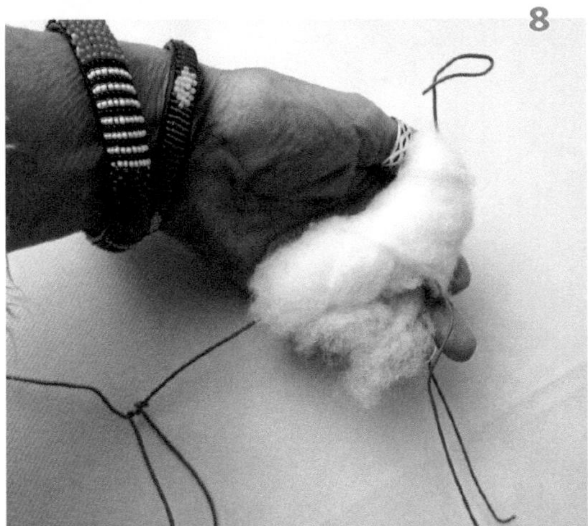
8

Continue to wrap around the neck, back, under the chest, etc, until you have used up the length of wool. Felt down tightly (as opposed to wrapping).

Step 7
10, 11

Now use another similar length of core to cover the other half of the body, by tacking it onto what you have already done and then wrapping it around the body, under the tail, back around the hips, under the tail again and back up the body. Wrapping under the tail will help to anchor the wrapping and keep it secure. Felt down.

You should now have a good and even wrapping covering the trunk of the body. If it isn't evenly covered, add a little more wool and felt down.

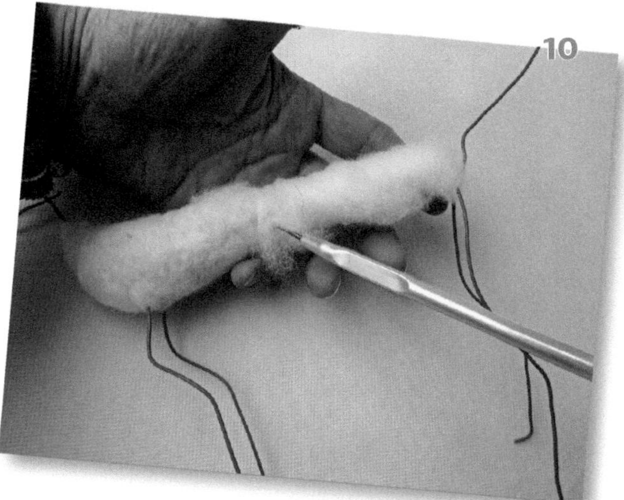
10

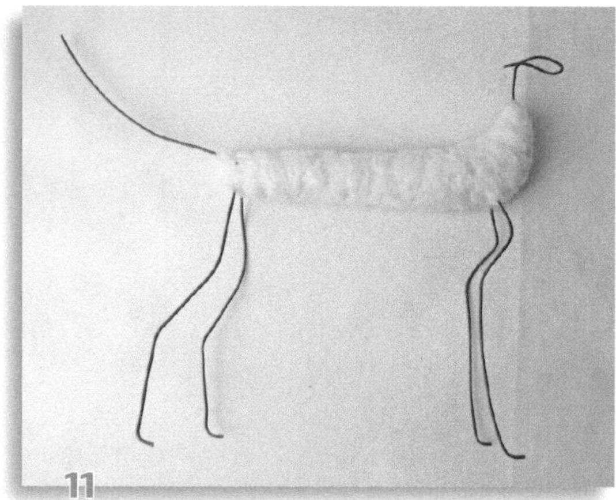

Step 8
12

To cover the legs, take a fine, roughly 20cm (7.87in) length of relaxed wool with a roughly 3cm (1.18in) thickness, and tack one end to the shoulder (you might find it helpful to gently part the front legs as you work on each one).

Now tightly and evenly wrap the length down the leg (aim to use half of the length to wrap to the paw; then the other half to wrap back up). As you wrap, hold the wound wool, letting go of the unwrapped wool so that it doesn't twist or kink as you wrap. You need a nice even covering of wool, without any twists or bumps, as these will be difficult to remedy later to make a nice smooth leg.

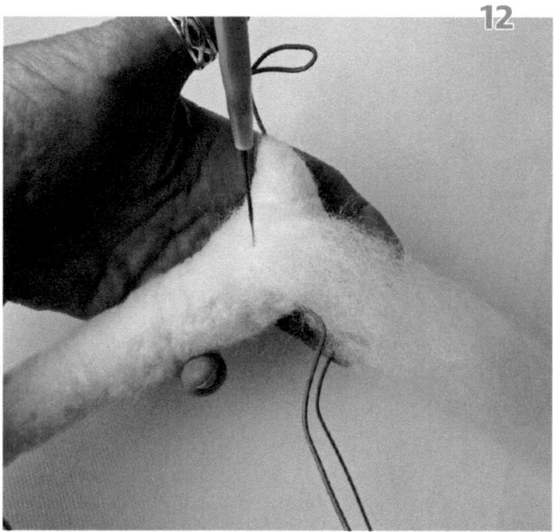

Step 9
13, 14

When you reach the paw, wrap only halfway and hold in place with one hand whilst you bend the exposed length of wire back onto the wrapped part of the paw with the pliers, and crimp it tight, so that it secures the wrapped wool in place. If your wrapping comes loose, you haven't crimped the wire tightly enough on the wool. Try again.

With the remaining length of wool, wrap back up the leg nice and evenly, finishing at the shoulders. Felt down in place.

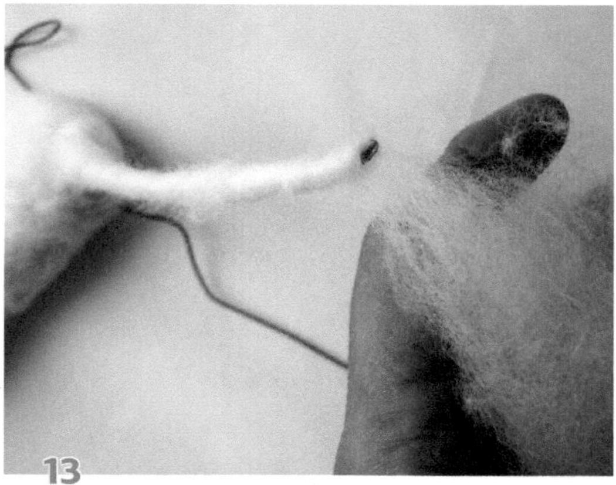

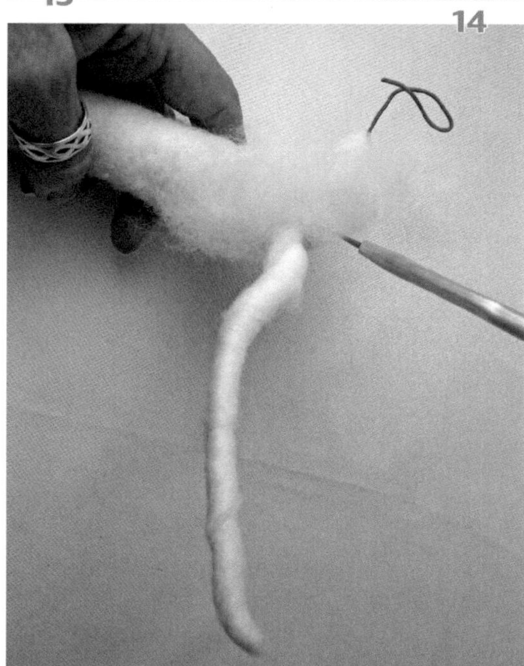

TIP
If the plastic coating comes away from the ends of the wire, simply trim it off

Step 10
15, 16

Wrap the remaining three legs and the tail in the same way, then wrap the neck and head. You don't need to secure the wool with wire for the head, just wrap up and back down again and felt down. Neck length should not measure more than 5.5cm (2.16in), as shown.

15

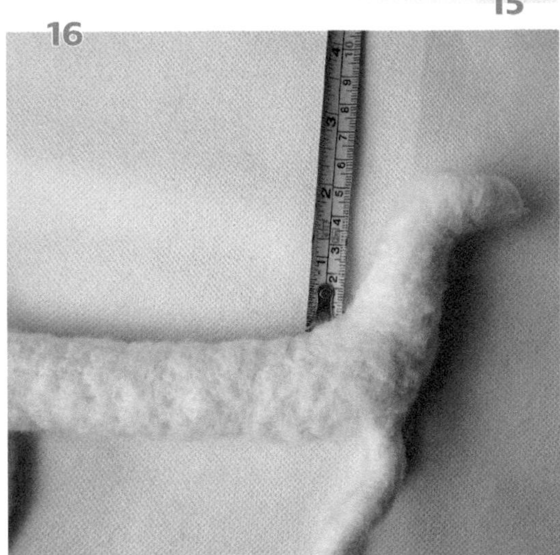

16

Step 11

Now go over what you have done and make sure that the armature can stand squarely and unaided. Re-shape if needed..

Step 12
17-19

To add bulk to the body, take two fist-sized pieces of white core wool and felt onto each side of the body, and down to the underside. Retain the top line of the sculpture, making sure you add bulk only to the sides and underneath, as the line has been created to be the final height of the dog.

Felt down fairly tightly. You won't see much shaping at this point; just a basically-covered body.

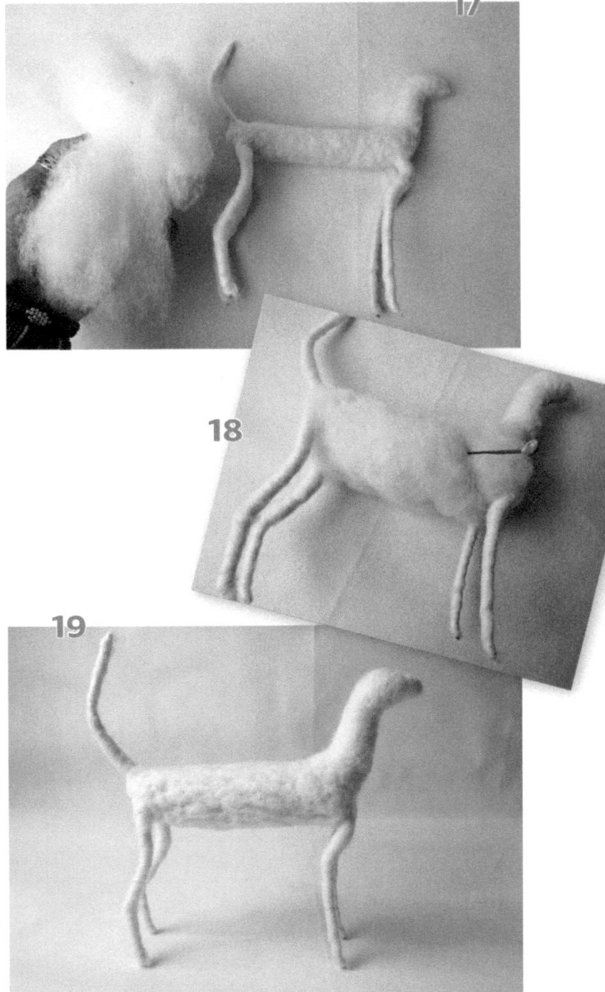

17

18

19

Step 13
20-23

Before you add any more shape to the trunk, add some bulk and shape to the tops of the legs.

For the hind legs tack a length of white core wool, similar in size and thickness (in loose fluffy state) to the trunk of your dog. Tack one end onto the hips and wrap under and around the top third of the back leg, then back around the leg once more and forward up towards the hips.

Don't wrap these additions as tightly as you did the initial covering as this looser covering will allow you to felt shape and form. Repeat for the other side.

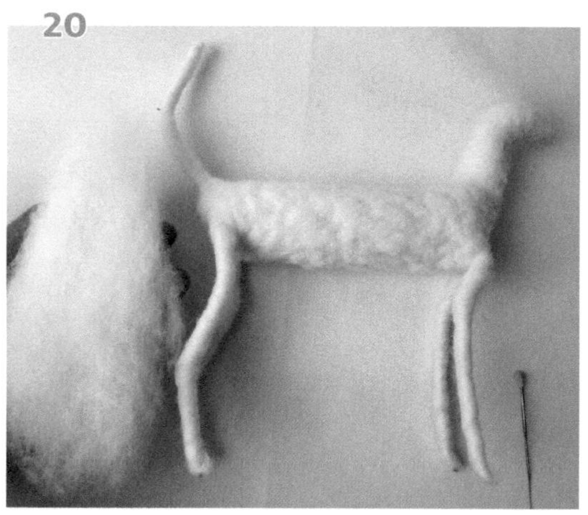
20

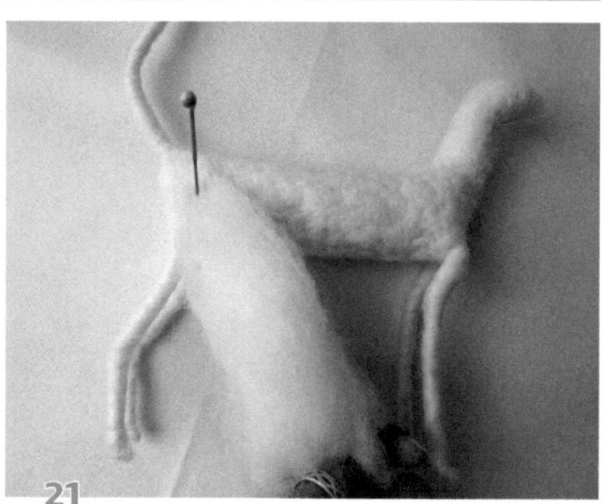
21

Step 14
24-26

Use the same process for the front legs, only with a shorter and finer length of wool. Start by tacking to the shoulder, wrap around the top of the leg as far as the elbow, back up again, and finish off on the shoulders, with shoulder and elbow shaping in mind as you lay the wool in place. Felt down.

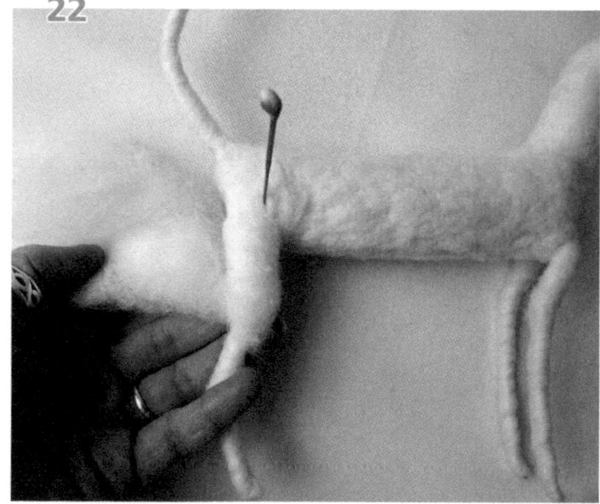
22

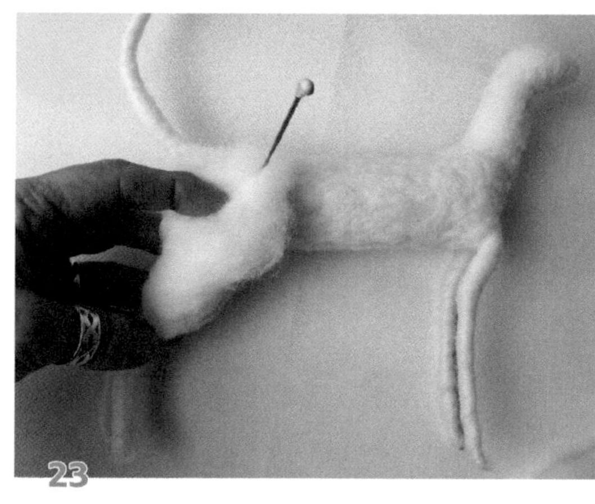
23

Step 15
27

Now add more bulk to the body, being mindful of the Chihuahua's shape and form. They have rather chunky bodies for the size of their frames, so be sure to

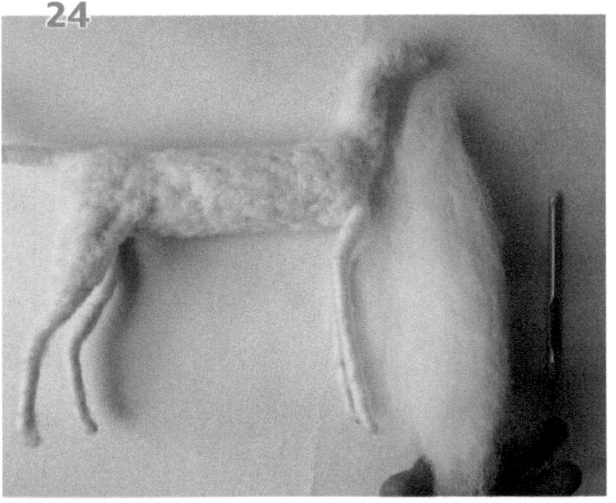
24

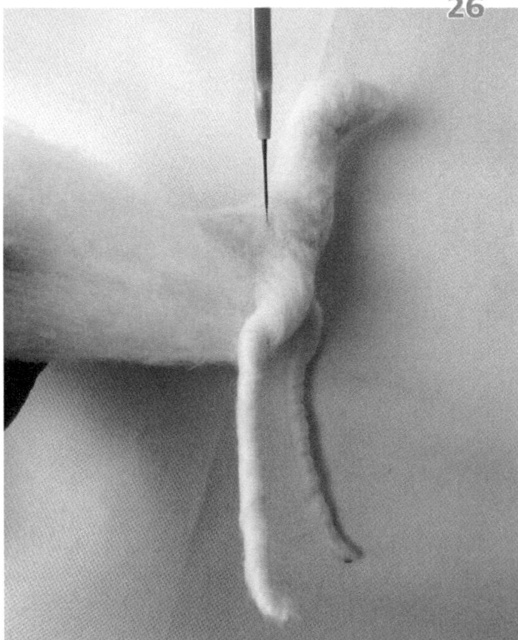
26

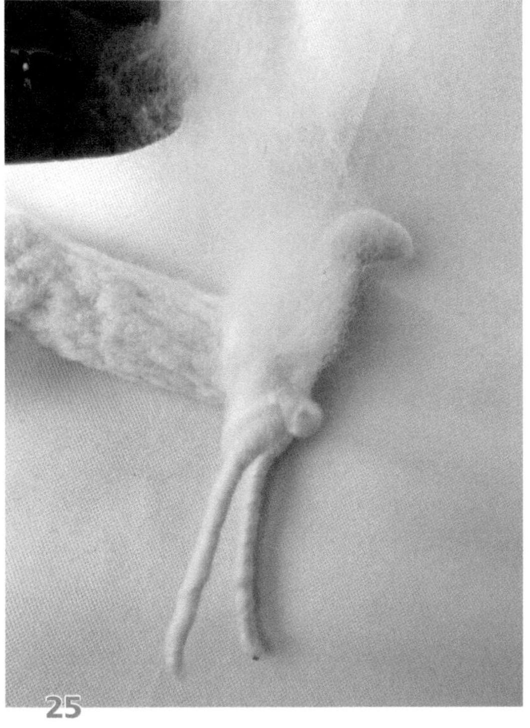
25

27

Google lots of photos from different angles. Add small amounts of wool and build up the shape rather than simply adding large bulk. More refined additions of wool will result in a far more professional finish, showing more detail.

Step 16
28-30

Give shaping to the legs by laying small amounts of white core on the leg and felted down into shape. Do not wrap, as wrapping at this stage will only make the wool taut and unsightly. Use a finer needle to work on the legs.

This is now the 'sculpting' process, not unlike sculpting with clay: assess where more shape is needed, add a little wool, and felt down into place and shape, using small amounts of wool each time. Also add more shape to the body, being aware that only a fine layer of wool will be required for colour, so you can make your Chihuahua's body shape as near finished as possible, because the fine coloured layer won't affect this.

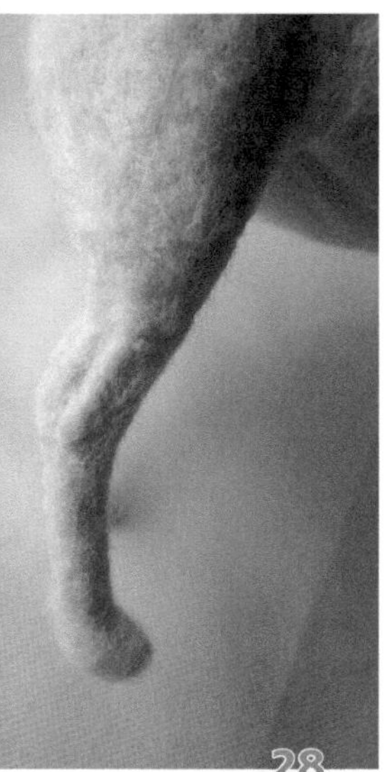
28

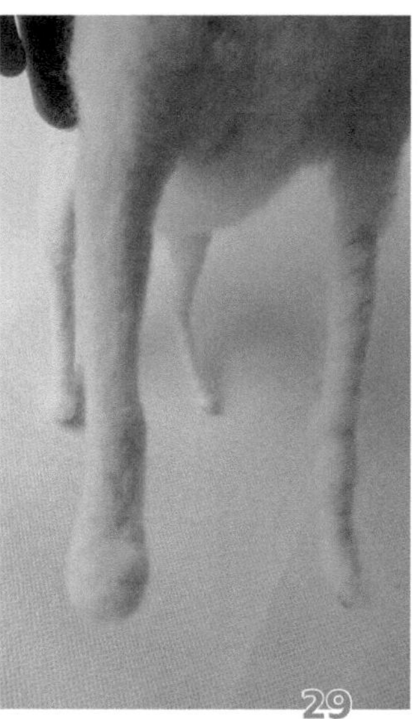
29

30

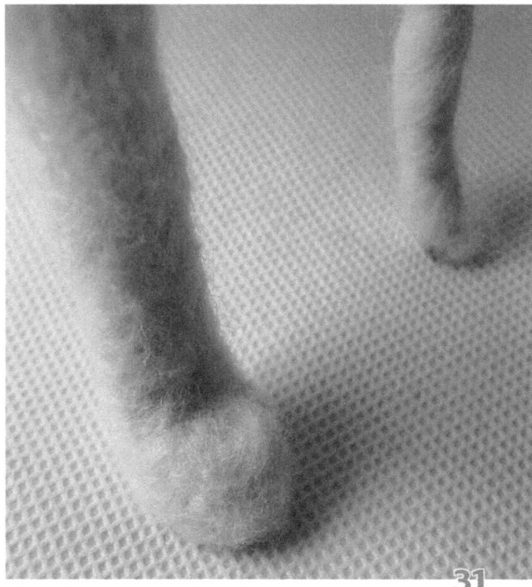
31

Keep inspecting the sculpture from all angles, and also check it can stand square and unaided.

Step 17
31

Fashion some generally basic-shaped paws, ensuring they are flat at the bottom (we are not making toes at this point, just a general paw shape). Chihuahua paws are rather pointed and a little narrower than other breeds of dog, and the hind paws are slightly smaller and narrower than the front, which are a little more splayed. Felt them fairly firmly: you probably won't get them right first time, and will need to adjust as you add the pads.

Step 18
32-34

Prepare the grey tops by cutting into 2cm (0.78in) lengths and hand carding each so that the fibres are fluffed up and have no straight edges. You can either felt the pads directly onto the paws, or mark them out with a Spectrum Noir pen, until you are confident with felting the pads. Using the pattern shown in the sketch below, start with the largest pad, moving on to the top two each side of the centre line, which can be easily placed, then the side two which, once the other three are completed, are easy to place. Felt a nice smooth surface to the pads and make clearly defined edges.

32

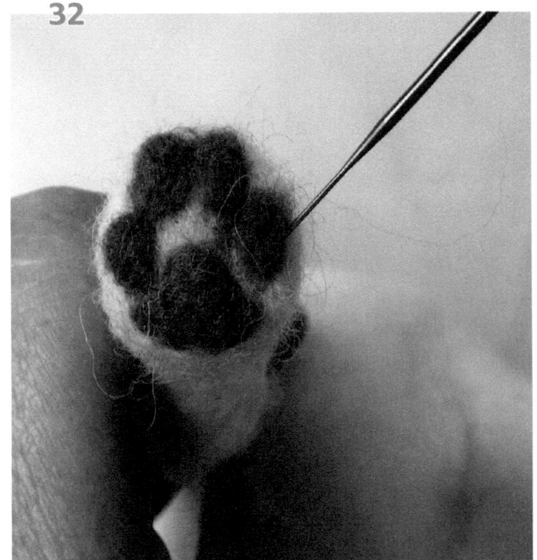

33

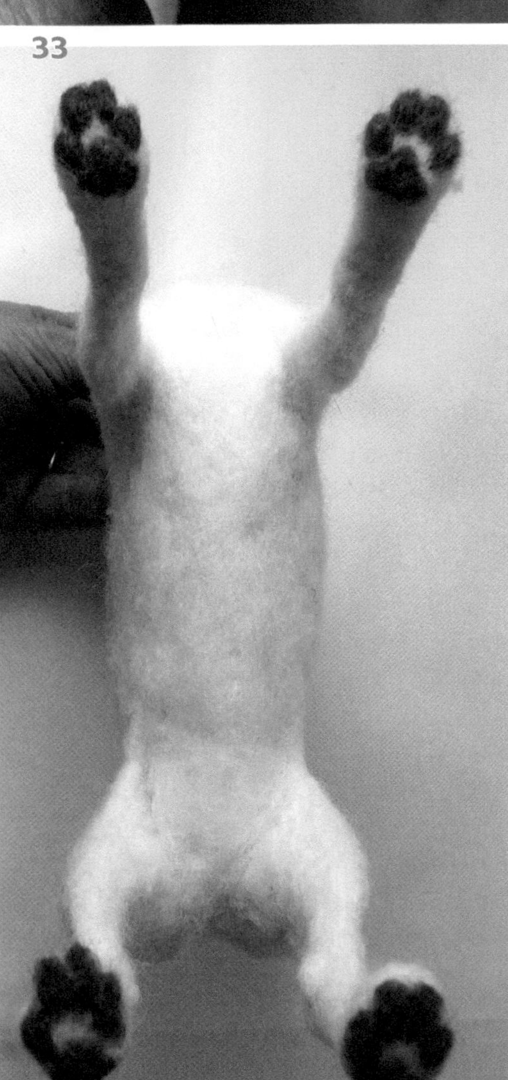

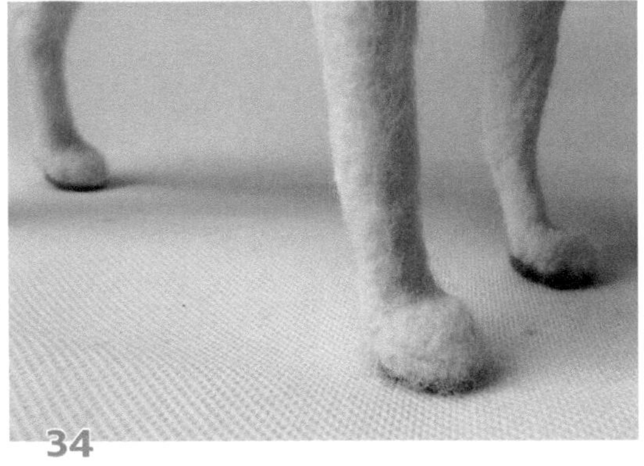

34

To help the pads bed into the paw so that they look as though they are growing from the paw and not on them, gently reverse felt the white core between them.

TIP

If you find that the pads are not fitting as neatly as they should, you may either be making them too large and so too wide, or you haven't made a wide enough paw. At this point you can easily add more paw at the sides with more core wool. As long as the pads are even and correct, they will help guide finer shaping of the paws

Step 19
35, 36

Now you are ready to separate the toes. Using small, pointed scissors, make the first cut between the two front toes. Start by placing the point of the bottom blade just underneath the paw between the front two pads, using these as a guide to where to cut between them. Then close

35

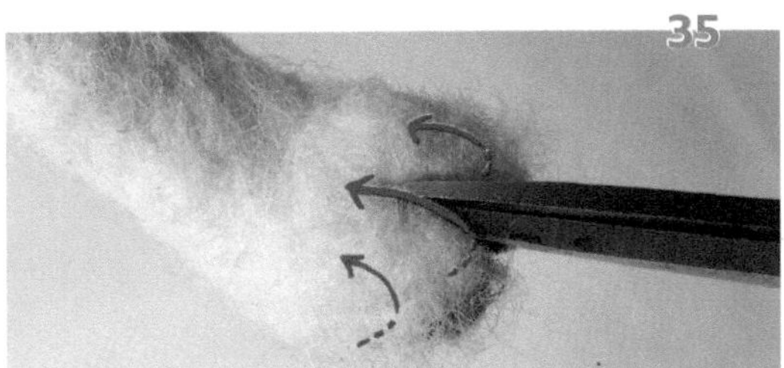

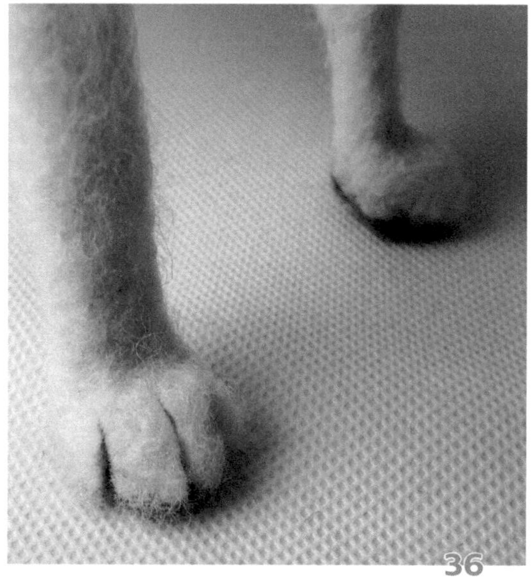
36

the blades over the top of the paw, in the line between the front two pads. Cut only halfway through the paw and not as far as the leg. Do the same for the other toes each side of each paw, also not cutting as far as the leg.

Step 20
37-39

Felt down the cut edges between the toes (you can also trim them a little first and then felt). Add some detail and definition to each toe, and adjust if needed where the pads show around the edges by covering with small attachments of core wool. You can very gently reverse-felt some white core to help cover the edges of the

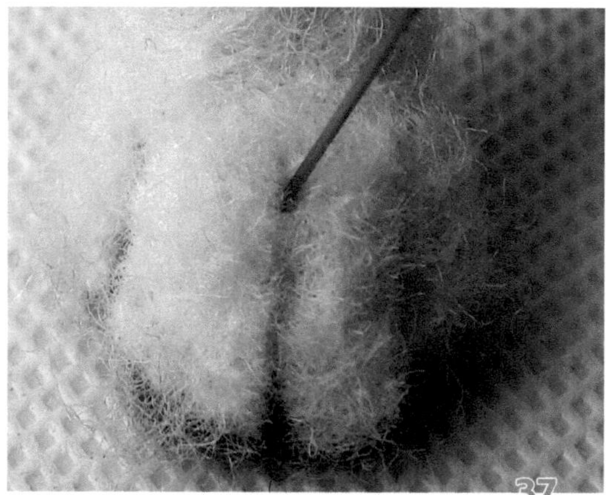
37

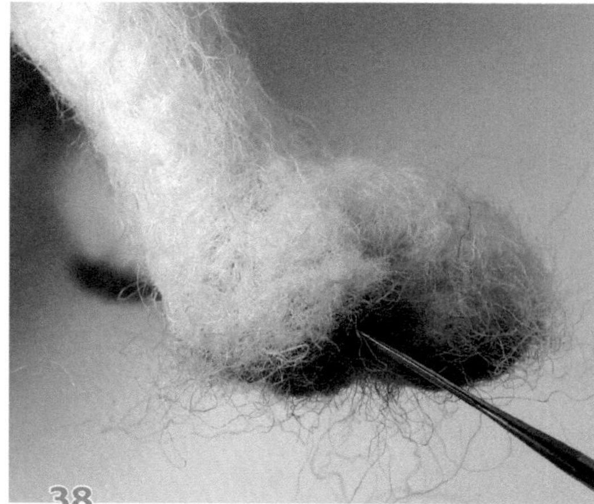
38

39

pads. Add a little more grey to the very front of the pads.

If you study dog paws you'll see that their pads actually show a little at the front, almost up to where the nails will be placed. This step is easier to achieve after the toes have been made.

Complete all four paws. You can, at this point, continue to add shaping up the legs from the paws to make them seamless.

Step 21
40

Check over the leg details, especially the hock joints on the hind legs and pasterns on the front legs. Assess the body shape, making sure that the hips are narrower than the shoulders when viewed from above. Add the dewclaw pads at the back of each front leg by felting on a small ball of grey tops and surround with white core.

40

41

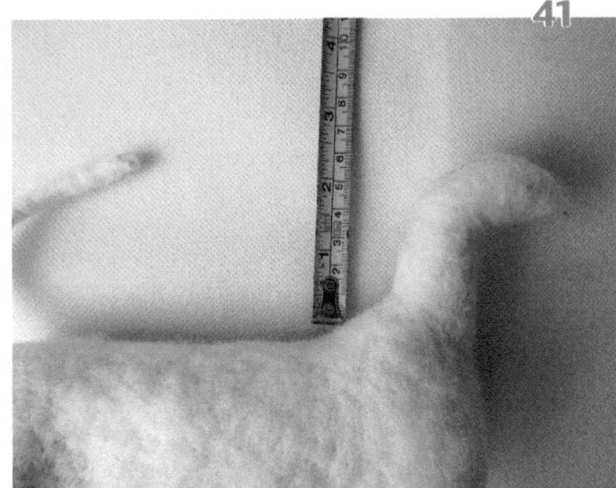

42

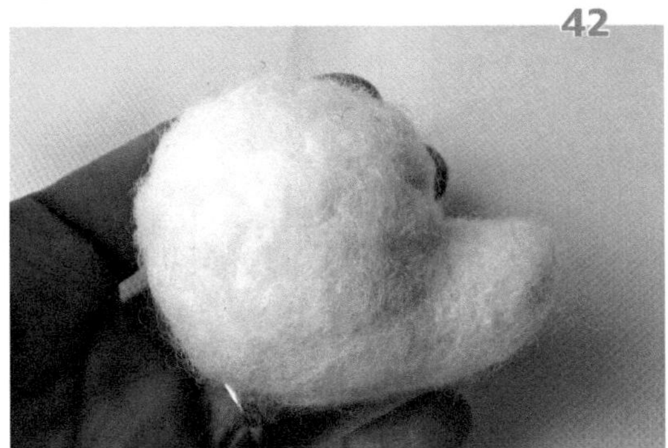

Add more refined shaping to the legs but remember to KEEP THEM THIN!

Step 22

41-45

Next is the head. Whilst measurements have been given for neck length, you might need to adjust this because how we each felt may differ, sizes and shapes will naturally vary, so check neck length before adding the head. Looking at photos of the Chihuahua, you will notice that head length (excluding the muzzle) is equal to neck thickness. Adjusting the neck measurement is very simple: you need only bend the head length over onto itself a little to shorten it; then make the bend between head and neck a little lower down.

To make the head, felt a ball roughly 5.5cm (2.16in) in diameter and shape

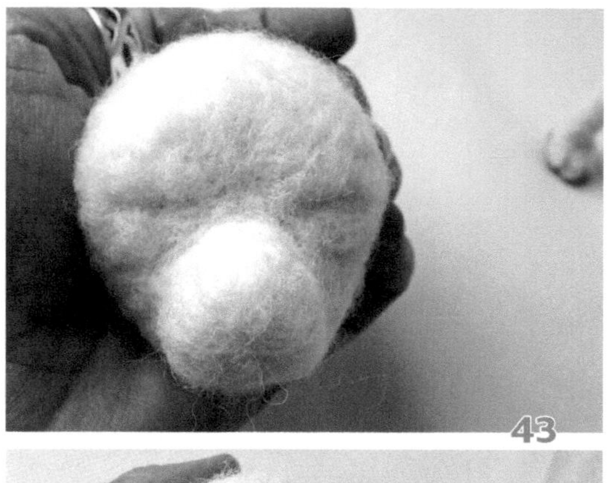
43

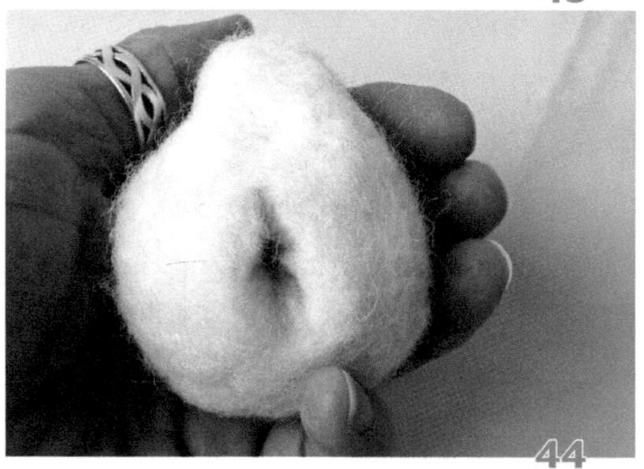
44

45

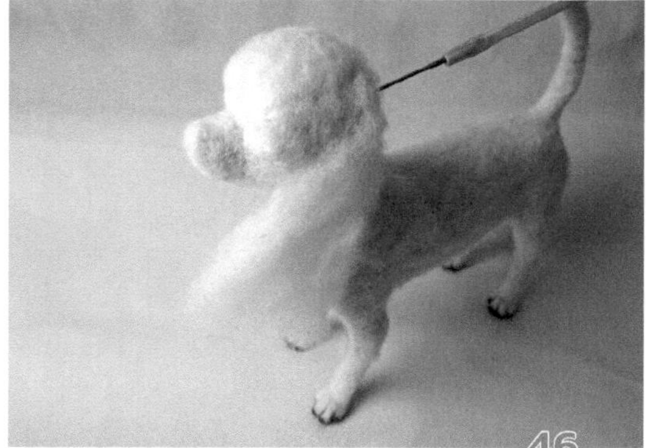
46

47

48

a small muzzle that sits halfway down the front of the head. Add extra wool to accommodate the eyes, as Chihuahua eyes actually protrude from the head, and felt a line where the eyelids will go. Don't felt down the head shape too tightly, as you need to make a cut in the base of the head. Offer up the head to the neck to gauge how it sits. If it's not low enough, cut the hole a little deeper (not too near the top of the head or where the eyes will sit), and/or lower the wire for the head a little.

Step 23
46-48

When you're happy with how it fits, tack a little wool onto the back of the head and place it on the neck. Felt down the wool to the neck and secure. Hold the head in place as you felt it on to prevent it moving and making the neck too long. Add small amounts of wool over and around the join so that the head is securely felted onto the neck. Add some more bulk to the neck, ensuring that the head is joined well with the body. Tack wool to the back of the head, wrap down to the front of the chest and felt down.

Do the same to the other side, remembering to hold the head in place as you felt down to a fairly firm touch. The head should now be fixed in place, and you can add more bulk around the neck, chest and tops of shoulders. Keep re-assessing your shaping.

49

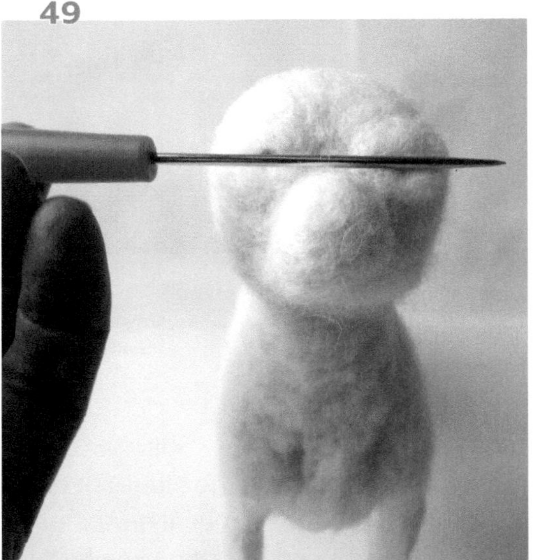

Step 24
49

Now to add more detail to the head and face. For reference, the lines for the eye positions will sit level with the bridge of the muzzle. Initially, we are going to fit 12mm (0.47in) 'spacer' beads and not the actual eyes. This is to create a stable cavity, into which the actual eyes can be easily offered; It also allows you to work around the spacer beads without scratching or damaging the finished items.

50

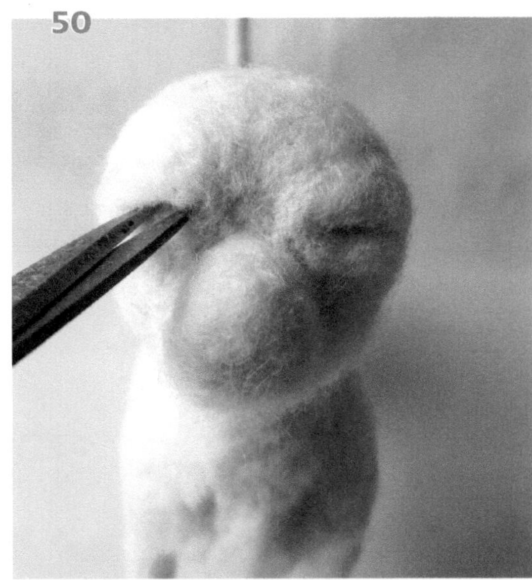

51

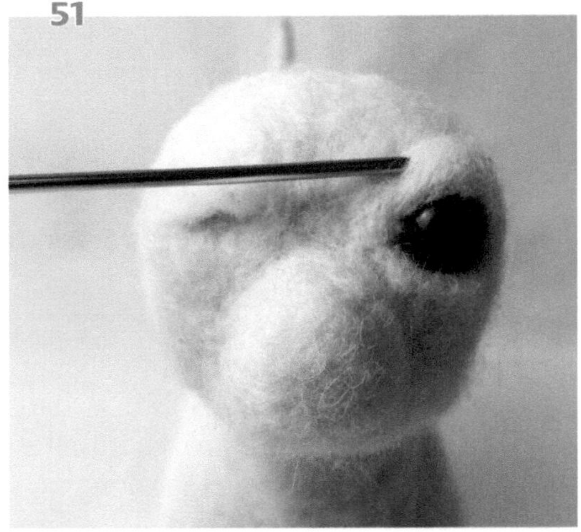

52

Step 25
50-53

Make a horizontal cut into both eye

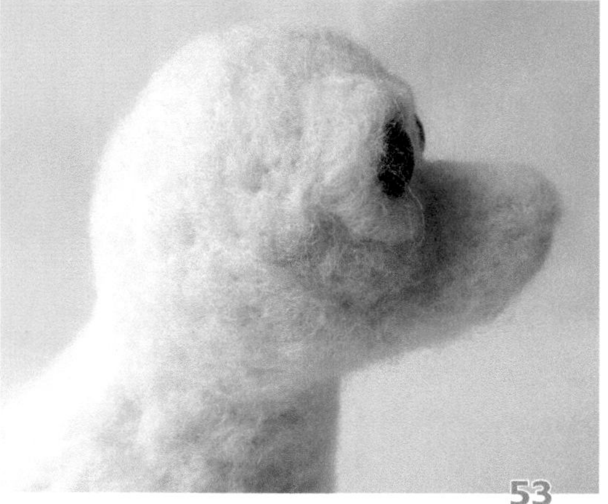
53

cavities, roughly 9mm (0.35in) deep and 9mm (0.35in) wide. With scissors, pen up the cavities until they are just wide enough to accept the spacer beads. Cut horizontally to help emulate a natural eye. Now use the awl to help fit each bead by gently pulling the eyelids over them: it should be a snug fit and the cavity should naturally hold the beads in place.

Now that you have fitted thc tcmporary eyes, work on shaping around the eyes and head. Define the eyelids by felting them a little thinner, ensuring they are equal in shape and size. Roughly one third of the eyeball should be showing, with the remaining two thirds inside the socket.

TIP

If you have cut too deeply into the eye socket, add a little wool to this and try again. Conversely, If you can't get the bead to fit in the cavity, cut a little deeper and wider, but cautiously. The beads should not be able to slot straight in, but neither should they be too tight a fit. Once a good cavity has been formed, popping eyes in and out will be easily done

Step 26
54, 55

Make a felted line/indent where the

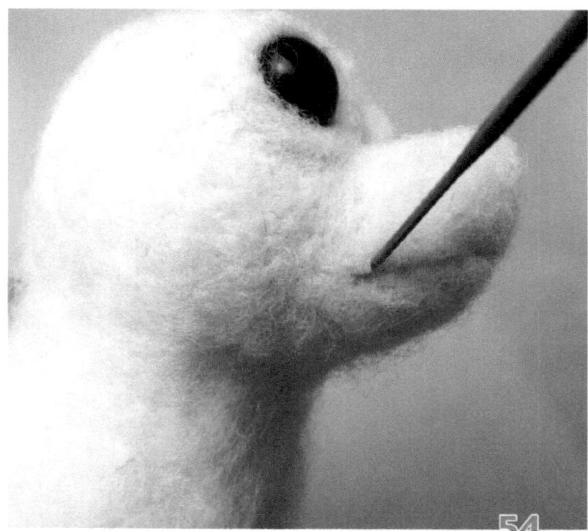
54

55

mouth will go, then make a shallow cut along the line to create the mouth details. Be sure to make the cut equal on both sides (why you need the felted line first). When you cut, do so with the plane of the scissors sloping downwards, as opposed to cutting at a 90 degree angle to the mouth:

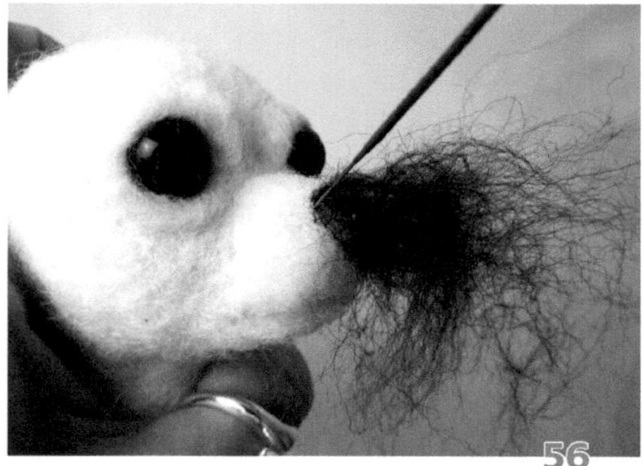
56

57

this will help to create a more realistic-looking mouth.

Step 27
56, 57

Add some black tops to fashion the nose. When you have felted a rough, soft (not tightly-felted) nose, mark two indents where the nostrils will go with the felting needle. Place two round-headed sewing pins into the nostrils until they are flush with the outside surface of the nose. Now add more wool and felt around the pin heads for more detail and definition.

> TIP
> **Whilst it might seem that the instructions flit from one unfinished part of the dog to another, it is often easier to work in this way in order to see the overall shape and proportions develop alongside one another. Often, a shape can only be defined once another shape or process has been completed first**

Step 28
58, 59

Once you have applied as much detail to the body as you can, colour comes next. Decide what colours you would like and mark out the pattern on your sculpture, on paper, or simply follow photos. This

58

59

Chihuahua is going to be fawn/tan. Map out where you will attach the tan colour and make a light covering, tacking it to the body. Try to keep the covering even, adding a little more as you felt the colour into the body so that the coloured wool mixes with and is felted into the white wool. You can use a multi-needle (not sprung type but open type) to do this on the larger areas. Take note that even Chihuahuas of a single colour have darker and lighter markings of that colour.

TIP

If you find a photo that you really like, but it shows only one side of the dog, you could use a photo app to 'flip' the photo to show the dog as if from the opposite side. Although, of course, the markings will be exactly the same, this means you can work on the markings of both sides simultaneously

Step 29

60

Once you have the colouring marked out and felted in, reverse-felt the colours to blend them into the white, in particular around the edges of the colouring and down the legs.

Using a fine reverse felting needle, gently and methodically reverse-felt along the outer edges of the colour. As you work, be mindful to do so in the direction of fur growth, pulling out the reverse needle in this direction. If you have felted in the colour enough, you should find the reversing works well, if you haven't felted in the colour enough, reverse felting will pull out the layer of colour.

Step 30

Reverse felting is time-consuming but shouldn't be rushed. You'll also need to add another layer of fawn/tan along the back and neck, and the top of the head, where the fawn is darker than on the

60

sides or underside. You will notice, as you reverse-felt, that the surface will become fuzzy, but don't be tempted to felt this back into the body. Instead, trim off the fuzz, but leaving that around the neck and underside, and back of legs. Even a smooth-coated Chihuahua doesn't have a coat that is all one length.

Reverse-felt along the tail, adding a layer of white core on the underside, and blend the two colours together along the sides. When you trim the tail, the top lengths will be shorter than the sides and underside.

Step 31
61-64

Before we apply any more detail to the head we will make some ears.

Using a felting brush and multi-needle tool (sprung type), felt a couple of flat triangles from fawn wool that measure 5.5cm (2.16in) wide and 5cm (1.96in) high. Ensure there is extra wool along the bottom edge (not part of the measurements given), which will be used to secure the ears to the head. Always use an awl to lift the ears from the felting brush, as pulling them off with your fingers will stretch them out of shape. Make sure you have a nice thickness – just enough not to see through the material – and felt both sides of the ears.

To tidy the edges, hold each ear between thumb and forefinger and, with a single needle, felt along the edges to create a

61

62

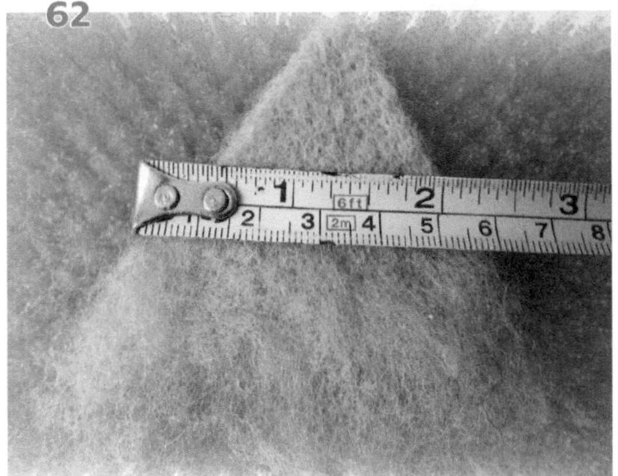

63

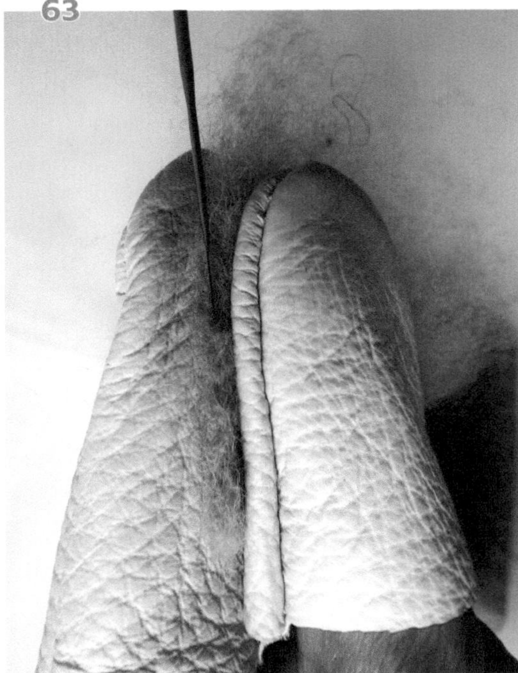

64

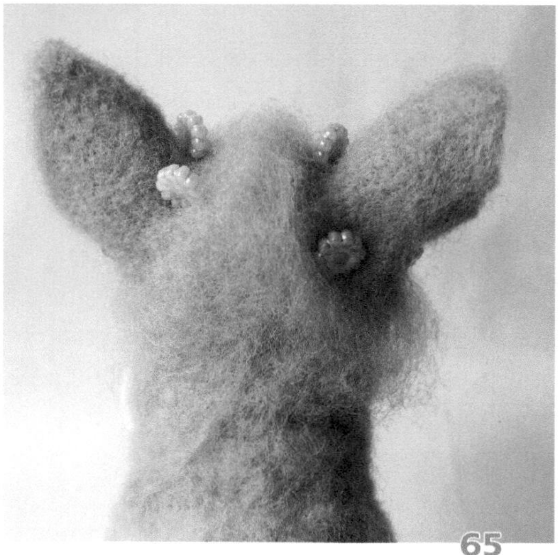
65

66

nice smooth edge (63). Trim along the top two edges when finished, and also gently trim along the surface of the ears, taking care not to trim too much and making them see-through.

Place ears back-to-back to check they are the same size and shape) Trim to shape as required. (64) shows one ear completed alongside another that isn't.

Step 32
65-67

Next up is fitting the ears. Using three large-headed pins for each ear pin into position on the head. You might, at this stage, need to add a little more bulk to the back of the head so that the ears sit nicely. The pins (each side of the ear and at the back) are useful to help set them in the right position, equally located. Keep checking the ears from all angles. Chihuahua ears do not point completely upright but stick out slightly, and also curve in on the inside. The outer edges of the ears are attached at a slightly lower level than the inner edges.

When you are happy with their positions, secure the ears in place by felting around the back of each in a semi-circle, below

67

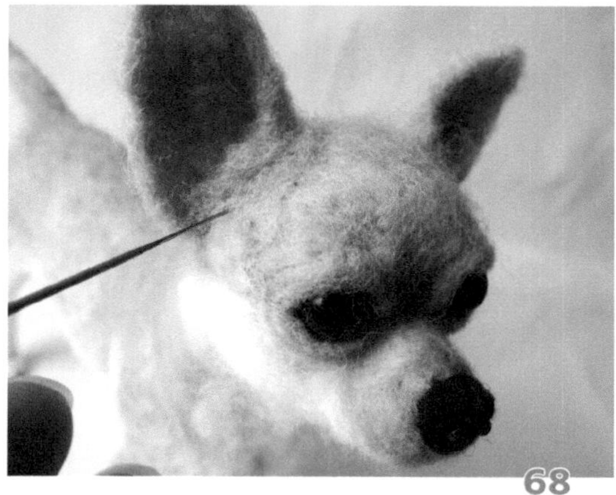
68

69

70

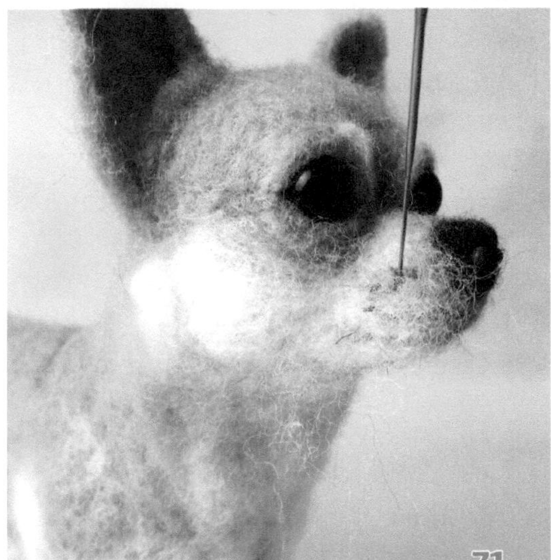

71

the pins. Felt down the allowed excess ear material at the bottom into the back of the head and neck.

Step 33

68

With the ears now located remove the pins. Add a little edging along the front of each ear with extra tan core. If you hold the ear between finger and thumb, you can easily and seamlessly felt this extra edging into the ear. Add a layer of tan core around the inside edge of each ear to felt into the bottom edge of the ear that attaches to the head to help secure the ear on the inside. This will also help the ears sit better.

Step 34

69-71

Continue adding more detail around the neck, and create an indentation for the jawline on each side of the head. Reverse-felt the colours on the head to blend them, and trim.

Chihuahua markings vary, as already mentioned, so be sure to study those you want to incorporate. To add some whisker detail to the muzzle, take a very fine wisp of grey tops and, with a fine needle, push into the muzzle in the opposite direction to that which the whiskers would grow. Continue to make three lines of these whisker markings, with four or five in a line. Trim the grey wool then apply a very light covering of white core to tone down the spots. The whiskers can be added at the end stage to ensure they don't become damaged whilst working on the sculpture.

Step 35

72-74

With the pins you placed in Step 27 in situ, give the nose a good surface trim to remove any fuzziness, then add a coating of Mod Podge, avoiding the pins whilst

72

73

74

keeping the lines clean and tidy around the nostrils. This will keep the nose fibre in place, and will provide a nice surface on which to build additional layers of Mod Podge. Once the Mod Podge is dry, remove the pins and felt into the nostrils to give some shape, and make a small horizontal cut each side of the nose, felt down the edges and trim. Add another coat of Mod Podge and leave to dry.

Gently file and smooth the surface of the nose with an emery board, repeating the process a couple of times until you have achieved the right texture for the nose. Before the final covering of Mod Podge, add some colour detail with acrylic paints if, for example, the nose has some distinguishing markings. With careful filing and coating it's possible to achieve a very good nose texture.

Step 36
75-78

A couple of ivory acrylic 12mm (0.47in) beads will make the eyes (ivory or off-white is a more natural colour than bright white). An awl threaded through the bead hole will secure the bead as you work on it, or you could use a length of wire threaded through the hole, with enough protruding to hold as you work. The important thing is that the bead is held securely and doesn't move about.

Using a circle template, place the 10mm (0.40in) circle over one eye, making sure to avoid the holes and any bead seams (the wire or awl will ensure this). Then, using the pointed end of a Spectrum Noir EB8 pen, completely colour inside the circle, using a circular motion, starting with the outer edge, paying particular attention to this and going over it a couple of times to ensure it is a little darker, continuing in a circular motion and working your way to

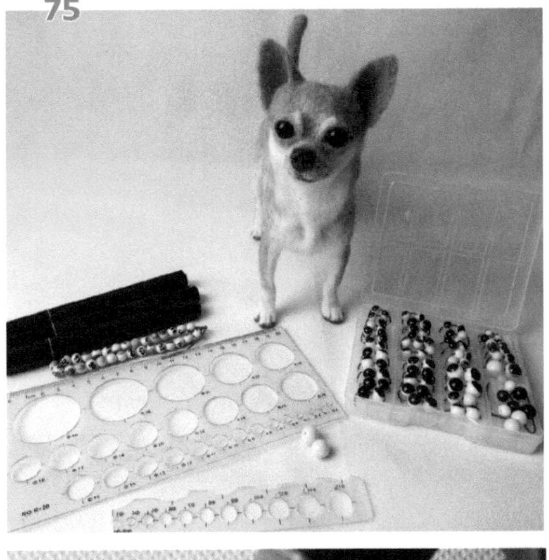
75

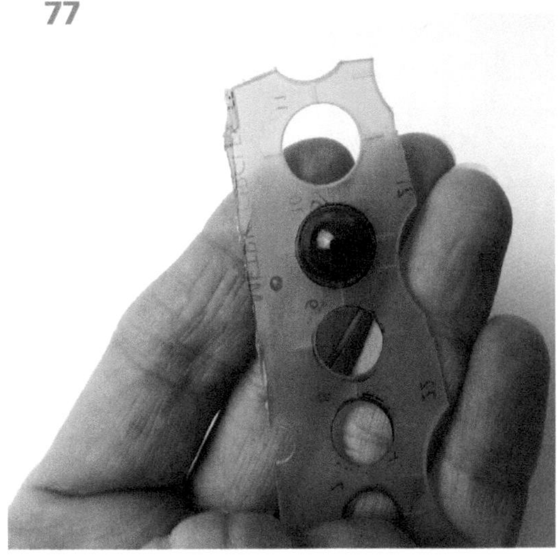
77

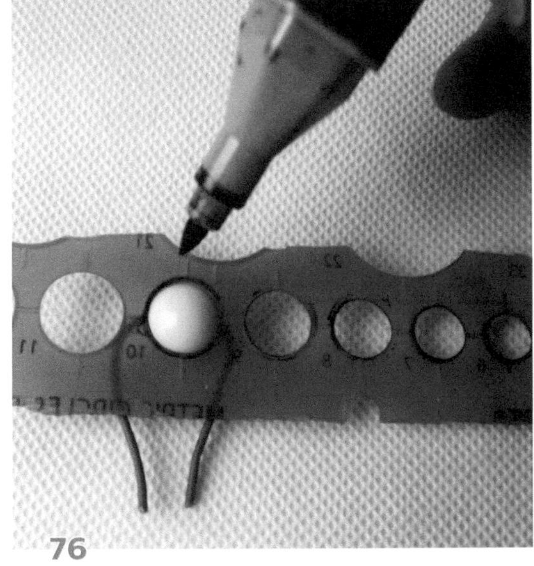
76

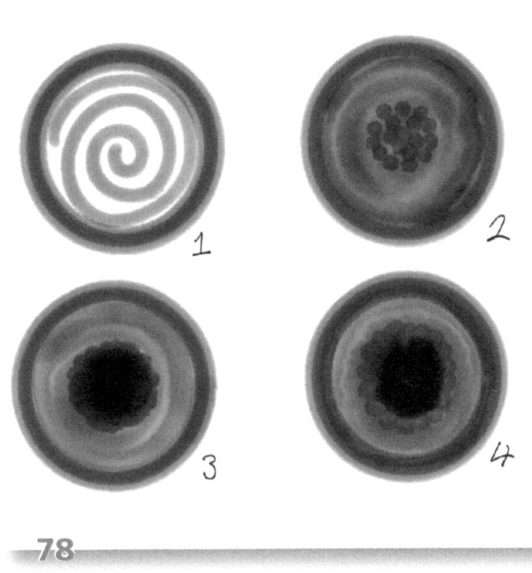

78

the centre. You will need to do this quickly, then immediately remove the circle from the template and allow to dry. If you colour a little and then allow to dry, subsequent pen strokes will simply wipe away what you have already done. Practice on some beads first, as there is a definite knack to it. Do this step quickly and decisively for each eye.

(78) shows the four steps of colouring.

TIP

Sometimes it can take a couple of seconds for the ink to flow properly if the pens have not been used for a while. For this reason, get them started on some practice beads. Also notice that some circle templates are bevelled, and will give a slightly different size on one side to the other, so be sure to use the same sides (clean the templates with a blender pen when done)

1 Initial colouring in a spiral pattern with EB8. The colouring will cover more of the bead than I have shown, but a circular motion is the best way to apply initial colouring. Use a Spectrum Noir blender pen to clean up any markings that have spilled outside the edges of the eyes

2 Where to dab the darker pupil colouring using EB8

3 Where to dab the black markings of the pupil.

4 Where to dab the brown colouring around the pupil edges to blend the pupil with the iris

Step 37
79, 80

Once you have applied initial colouring with EB8, dot the pupil area with the same pen. Allow to dry and then give the eyes a covering of Glossy Accents or Diamond Glaze: do this with a damp brush and be aware that it dries quickly, so apply with two or three decisive strokes only. Dry. With a black Spectrum Noir pen, make a pupil in the centre of the brown circle by marking out the pupil by dotting the very end of the tip very gently in a circular shape, and not by drawing a circle. Note that dog pupils are not normally very clearly defined, and blur into the iris, so ensure that, where your pupil markings meet the iris, the line is blurred. Check they are the same size. Allow to dry completely.

Now add another coating of Glossy Accents or Diamond Glaze, which are water-based and dry crystal-clear.
Once dry add more colouring over the Diamond Glaze coat by dotting over the line where the brown meets the pupil with the Spectrum Noir pens: blend/layer further without marring what you have already done. Finish off with another coating of Glossy Accents as this can add depth to the eye colouring and cover any imperfections. If feeling brave, try adding another couple of layers of Glossy Accents or Diamond Glaze to give the eye a convex lens-like effect. Allow to dry completely between each application.

Remove the spacer beads and gently colour the inside edge of each eye socket with the black Spectrum Noir pen. Don't be tempted to run the pen around the socket, but gently dab it along the edge to make a nice thin but even line, not disturbing the felting already done. You need make a fine

79

80

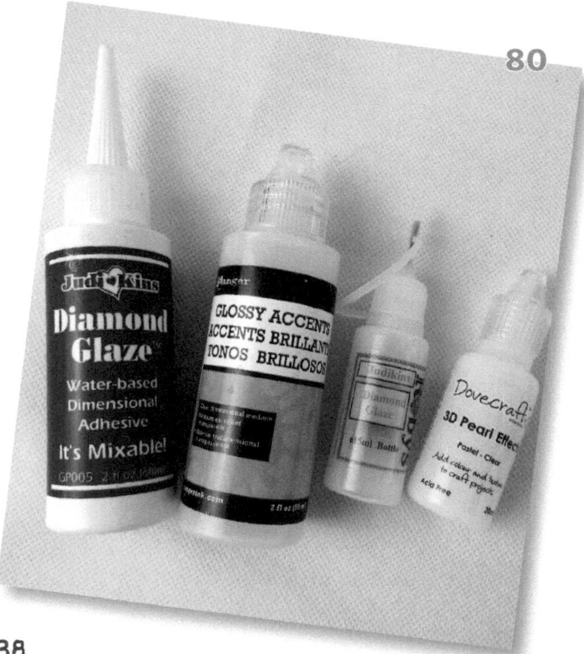

line only: enough to be noticeable when you replace the spacer beads with the real thing. Allow the ink to dry.

Don't be tempted to fit the completed eyes in at this point, because the ink could well mark them. It was precisely when making this mistake myself that I discovered that alcohol pens will colour off-white beads, which I was using as spacer beads to create the eye socket. It was definitely a eureka! moment in my needle felting journey ...

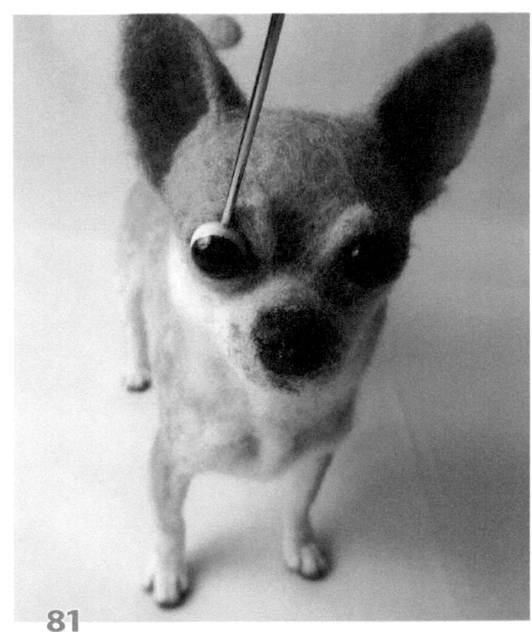

81

Step 38
81, 82

With the eyes now completed they're ready to fit, which should simply entail swopping these with the spacer beads. Check for socket size, and that the eyelid fits nicely, just covering the top and bottom of the iris, as shown in image 82. The outside corner can show some white of the eye. Adjust the eyelids as necessary, substituting the spacer beads if you need to work on the eyelid.

82

When satisfied all is correct, apply a small dab of PVA glue to the inside of the eye socket, and carefully fit the finished eyes, ensuring that the coloured part doesn't touch the glue at any point, and that they are correctly rotated and showing some white at the outside corners. Check and re-check that the eyes are in the correct position by looking from top, bottom, and both sides. You will have a little time until the glue sets to play with gaze direction, to ensure there are no squints or astigmatism. Leave glue to set completely.

83

At this stage any poking with the needle around the eyes will cause them to move, and also coat the needle with glue. There shouldn't be any need to make any adjustments to eyelid position or shape at this stage, in any case, as this should have

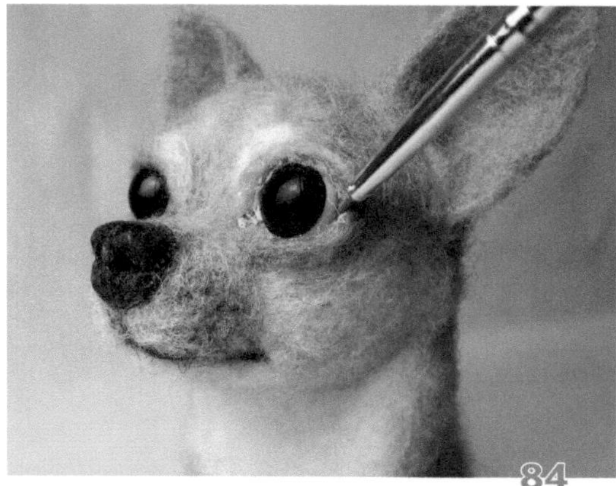
84

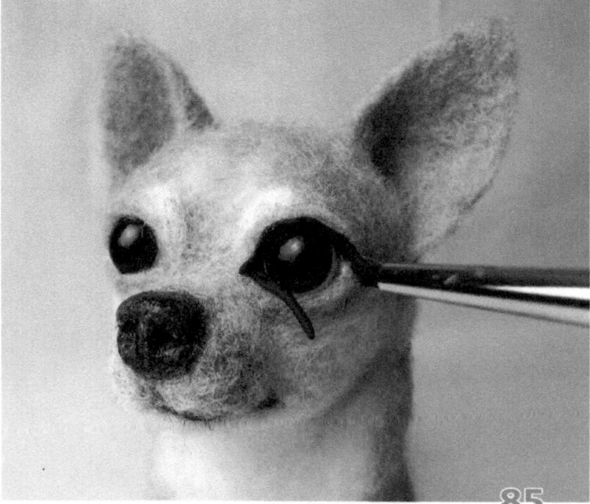
85

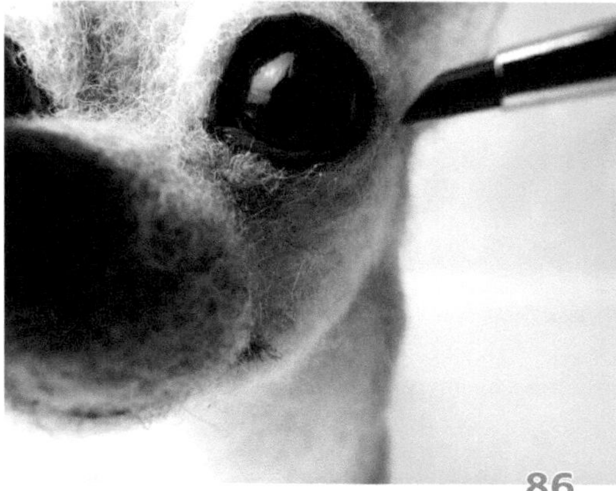
86

been completed when the spacer beads were in place.

Step 39
83-86

To complete the eyelids add some clay around the eyes. Silk Clay is perfect for this as it air-dries, and is easy to manipulate into place. You will need: dark brown Silk Clay, Gloss Mod Podge, a fine paintbrush and some small, rubber-tipped clay tools, plus a clean surface on which to roll the clay.

First, apply a line of Mod Podge to the eyelid, using the black ink line you made as a guide (work on one eye at a time), making sure you get into each corner of the eye. Work quickly from this point as such small amounts of Silk Clay will cure quickly.

Roll a small, pea-sized amount of Silk Clay into a thin and even length of approximately 1mm to 1.5mm (0.04-0.06in) thick, and cut to two lengths of approximately 2.5cm (0.98in), with one slightly longer than the other (the top eyelid). Place the longer length along the top eyelid, and gently mould it into the eye surround, to achieve the effect of skin on the edge of the fur-line of the eyelid. When you have the length of clay in place, push into the corners with your rubber-tipped pointed tool, and gently and evenly mould the whole length in and slightly under the wool eyelid without making any unsightly indentations with the curved, flat-tipped tool (this takes a little practice). Trim excess length at the corners of the eyes.

You can also gently push down on the eyelids with your thumb. Make sure you push them back far enough to show a little white of the eyes at the outside edge.

With the top eyelid done, attach the bottom eyelid in the same way. When finished, this will look rather large and bold, but most of it will be covered later. Make the clay eyelid as smooth and even as possible, with a very slight gap between it and the eyeball, which is achieved with the curved, flat-tipped tool.

Check that both eyes are equal by looking at your sculpture from all angles. Adjust as needed, and allow to dry.

TIP

Don't be tempted to return unused Silk Clay to the pot, but instead, roll it into lengths of around 1.5mm (0.06in) thick and cut into 5mm (0.19in) lengths to use as claws for future dog paws, rounding one end of each length into a blunt point and making the length slightly curved. Dry and store. Also before storing your Silk Clay, dip your finger into some water and wipe the surface before closing the lid. This will help keep your Silk Clay in supple condition. From time to time, remove the Silk Clay from its pot and work some water into it, a drop at a time, to make it fresh and soft again, then wrap in cling film and pop it back into its pot

Step 40
87-93

To cover some of the Silk Clay to make it look as though the eyelids are under the fur and not on top of it, build up between the eyelid and surround with core wool. You can do this by reverse felting, or by gently adding wisps of core wool around the eye and felting them in: a fine needle will make this possible. Take care not to damage the Silk Clay. Trim away any fuzziness to make a smooth blend.

Now add final colouring and detail to the face with a combination of pastels, and/or Spectrum Noir pens. Darken around the eyelids, especially the bottom and inside corners; maybe adding a tear stain. Other darkened areas are under the nose. Add your colouring lightly. Pens used for this project are GB9, TN7, EB6, RB3 and true black. If you feel you have added too much colour, tone it down by adding a

87

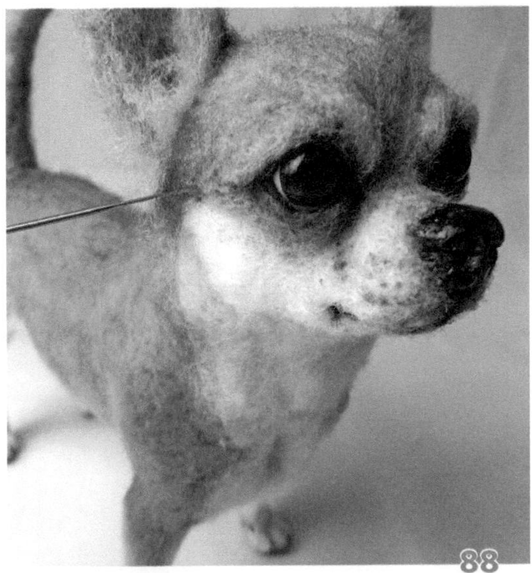

88

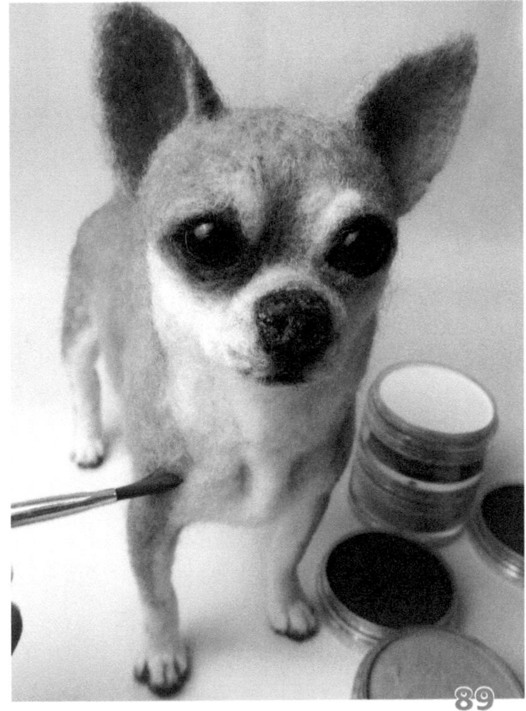

89

90

92

91

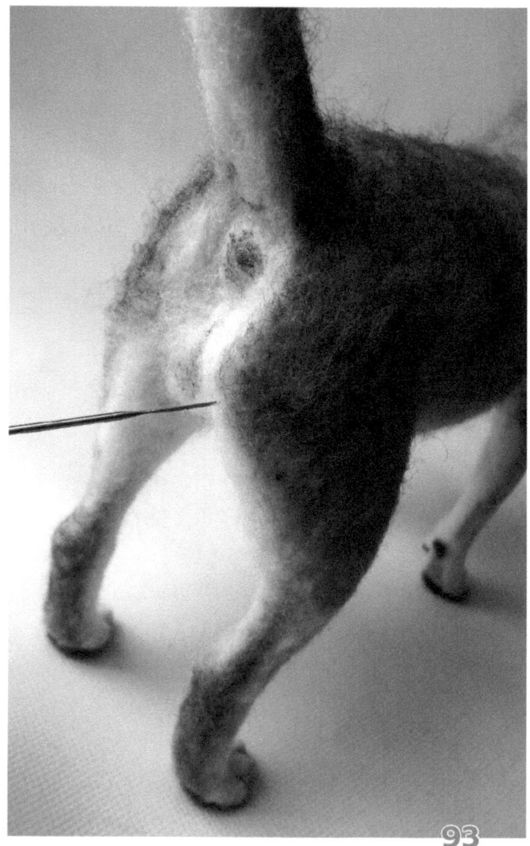
93

thin layer of fawn/tan or white wool over the colouring. 'Layering' is a useful and effective technique with which to create realistic colouring.

Continue to add colouring detail to the rest of the body. Pan Pastels are very effective for colouring detail, and, with a soft brush, can be added to areas where the coat is slightly darker, such as along the back, down the shoulders, the top and sides of the head, down the front legs, and on the sides of hind legs, etc.

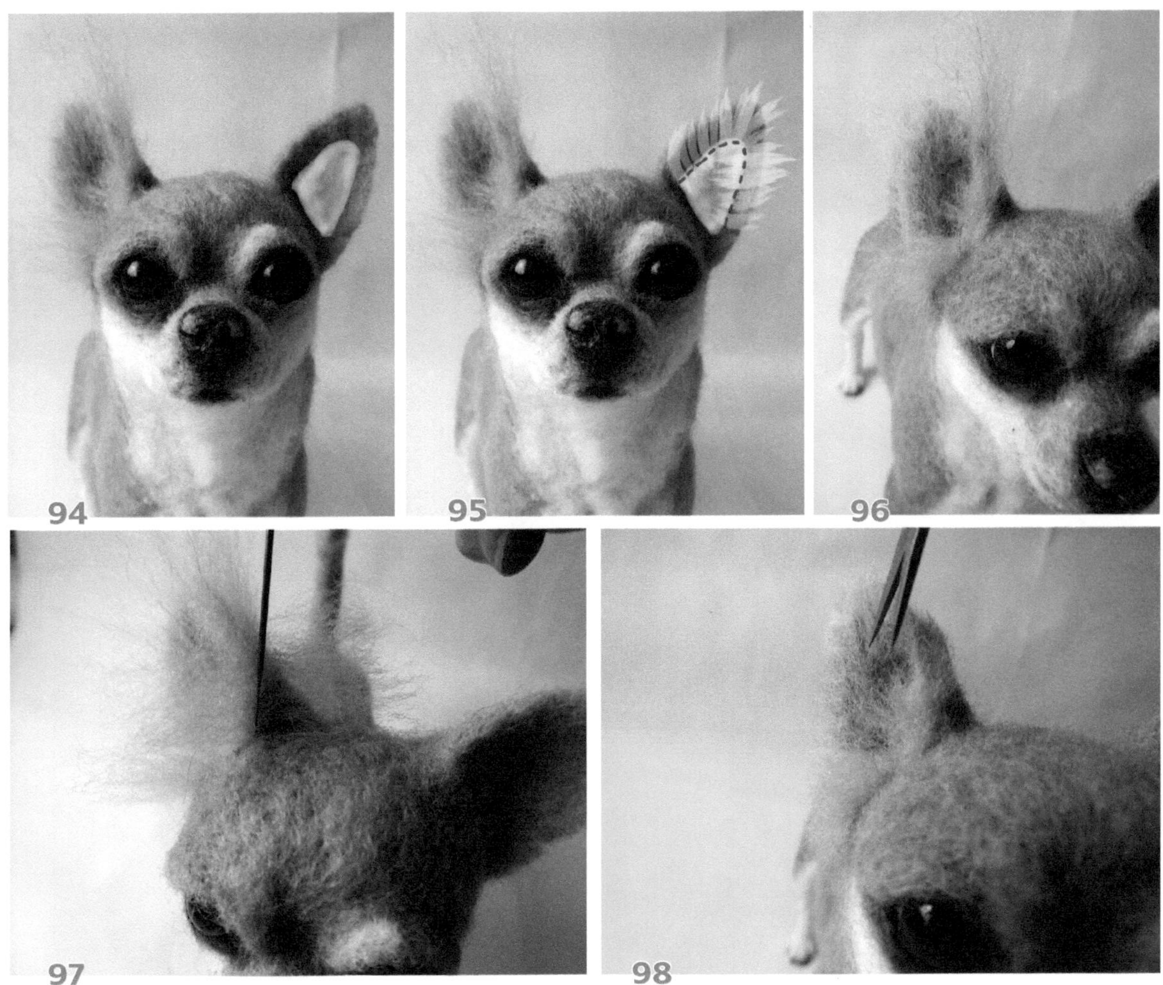
94 95 96 97 98

Step 41
94-98

To add fur and colour to the ears, colour the inside of the ear pale pink with soft pastel, leaving a good margin around the edge. Along this edge felt in a light covering of white core in wisps that overlap the pink, and cover the outer edge of the ear.

Felt down the white core into the ear along the red dotted line, and very gently over where it lays on the outer edge to secure it. Trim to shape around the edges. Gently and carefully reverse-felt and blend the edges of the ear where the white core meets the ears, with the aim of fuzzing-up the very edge of the ear so that it blends with the white core.

Trim the edges again, then add fawn/tan core around the front and a little way up the sides of the ear and around the front, so that it looks like longer fur. When using small amounts such as these, stretch the core to make it longer and straighter. Trim to length and add colour detailing along the front of the ears, where the markings would naturally be darker, using a combination of Pan Pastels and alcohol pens.

Step 42
99-103

One method to make the small nails and pad on the front legs is to first prepare the paw for the nails to be attached. Lightly colour between the toes with BG6 to

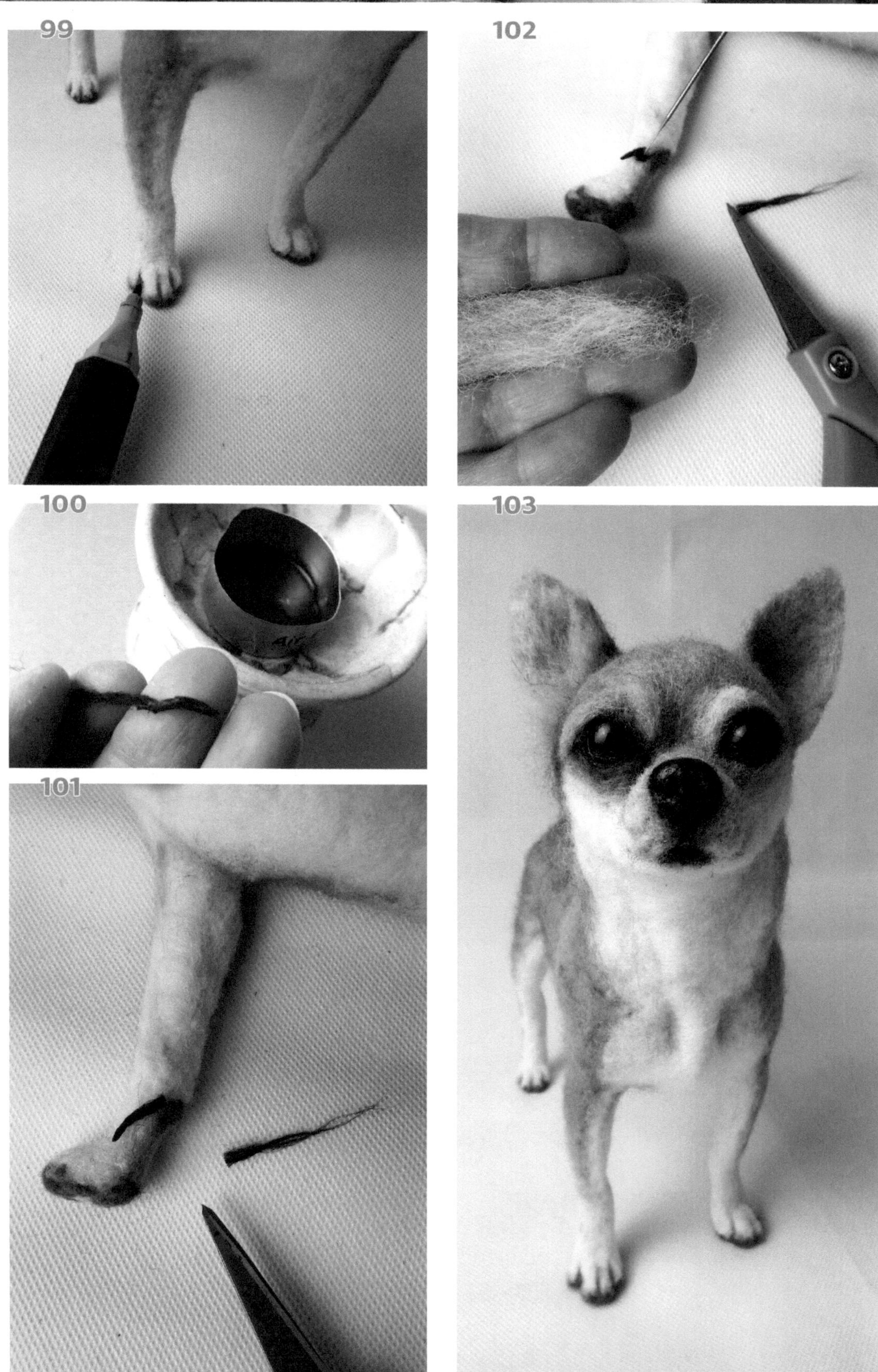
99
102
100
103
101

give the impression of depth and colour variation, and also take the colouring up from the pads to the tips of the toes. To create the nail for the inside claw, take a small wisp of black core wool, roll it into a string shape and dip it into black felting wax. As it cools, roll and shape it to make a claw. Cut to length and place on the inside of the leg alongside the pastern joint. Take some core white and place it over the top of the nail, then felt into a pad shape to make it appear that the nail is growing out of the pad. Trim to shape.

Whilst you have the hot black felting wax, give the nose a covering of this (103). You can use a brush but this tends to clog up quickly, so I use a metal clay tool. Gently heat the metal tool to reshape the wax on the nose once cooled. The felting wax can add a nice finish to the nose, or you can leave it with just the Mod Podge/filed covering.

Step 43
104-108

For another method to make the nails (ready to attach later), that are a particular feature of the Chihuahua, you will need some polymer clay. The colours used here are, FIMO flesh light, FIMO raspberry, FIMO translucent, FIMO white and FIMO black. White dog nails aren't just white, of course, as they often show the pink cuticle inside, especially with breeds such as the Chihuahua, who tends to have long nails.

To achieve this effect, roll some translucent FIMO to around 2cm (0.78in) in length and 2mm (0.07in) thick, then roll flat to make a width of around 1cm (0.39in). Mix two parts flesh light to one part raspberry with two parts white and blend well. Roll to a 2mm (0.07in) thickness and cut lengths of about 6mm (0.23in); then place two lengths of pink FIMO on to the translucent FIMO with a space between

104

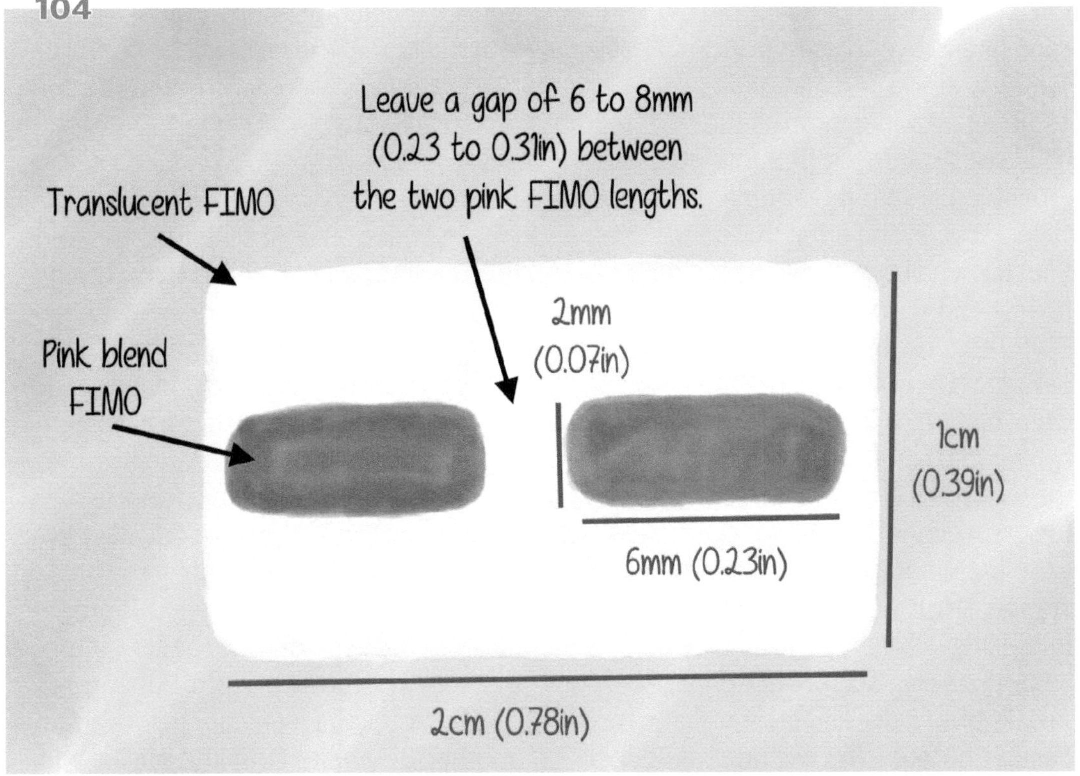

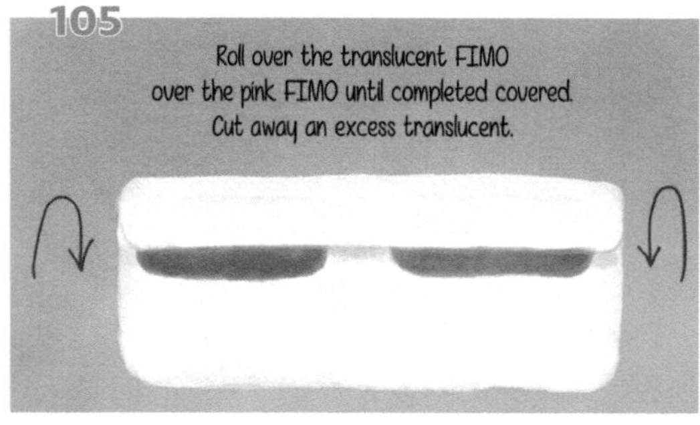

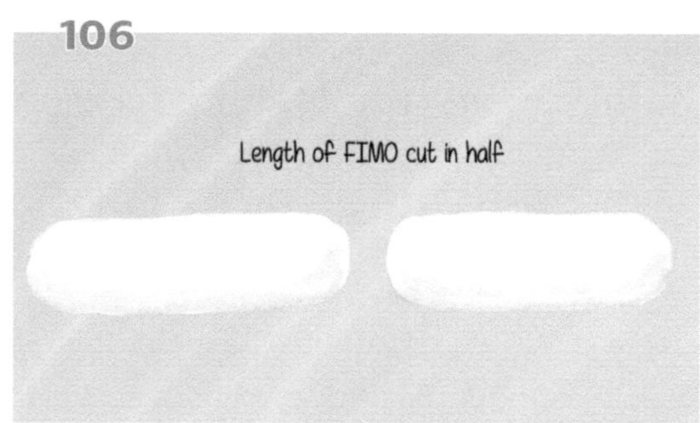

of 6-8mm (0.23-0.31in), as shown. Then roll the two pink FIMO lengths so that it completely covers the translucent FIMO. Cut away any excess FIMO .

Cut in half and gently roll the ends you have just cut into blunt points which will form the nail with the other end the pink cuticle that will be fitted into each toe. With each nail gently rolled to a blunt point, bend slightly into a natural curve. Place them on a piece of foil, ready for baking. Make at least 25 to 30 of these white nails at slightly different sizes as the two middle nails are usually thicker than the two outside nails. Bake at 130°C (250F) for just six minutes. The translucent FIMO will discolour if baked for too long as they are very small pieces, and don't need the full baking time.

Roll out some black FIMO to make 10-15 nails of similar size. Never make 'just enough' because you will need a range of sizes to choose from to suit each toe. Bake at the same temperature and for the same length of time. The nails will be fitted last as they are easily damaged whilst working on the sculpture.

Step 44

Finally, look over your sculpture and add further detailing or colouring you feel it needs. You can also give the eyes a final coating of Glossy Accents, but be sure to first brush these with a soft dry brush, and ensure there are no stray bits of wool on or in the eyes, as this will be glaringly obvious when the glaze has dried. Scrutinise the eye surfaces and be sure to cut away every stray bit of wool before adding the final coat of gloss. You want a nice smooth finish to the eye. You can paint on more than one coat to add depth, but ensure each coat is completely dry before adding another. Be sure to gloss the eyelids, too.

109

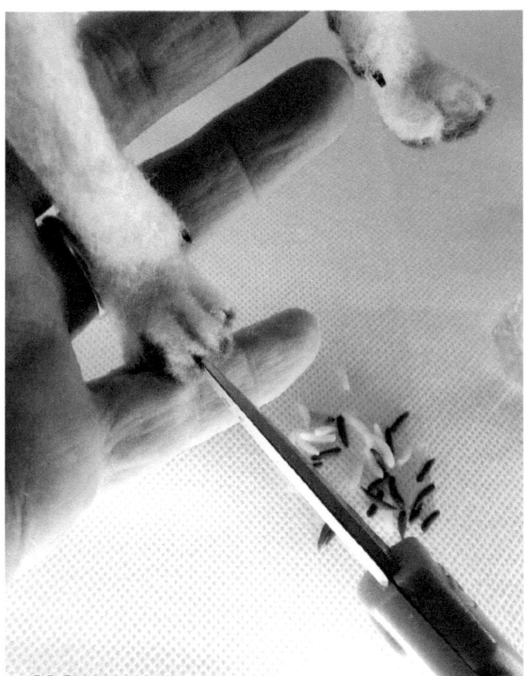

110

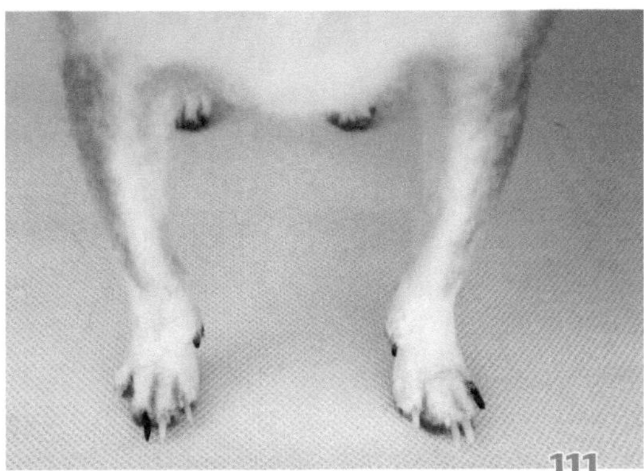

111

Apply the Glossy Accents with a damp brush.

Step 45
109-111

To fit the nails, cut a small vertical slit in the front of each toe (about half the depth of the nail being fitted), slightly offset to the top. As you begin to remove the point of your scissors, twist them 90 degrees inside the slit and open the blades slightly to make the opening wider, ready to accept the nail. Decide which nails are going into which toe, ensuring that the largest ones are paired with the middle two toes and the smaller ones the outer toes. Firstly, fit the nails dry to make sure they look right, are in the right place, and the cut is deep enough to take the nails correctly. Notice that the two middle nails on each paw are closer together than the outer nails. A common mistake is to evenly space the nails on the toes, which is incorrect.

Push each nail into place (pink ends into the toes) before adding glue. This not only opens up the cavity, it also demonstrates whether a deeper cut or better fit is required, without everything being contaminated with glue.

When you are happy with the fit, dip the end of each nail into some clear-drying PVA craft glue or Tacky glue and push into place; position and leave to dry. It's probably best to tackle one paw at a time, leaving it to dry completely before moving onto the next. It's all too easy to dislodge the nails as you move the sculpture.

Repeat for the remaining paws.

Step 46
112

To add some whiskers, using a carpet needle (essentially a curved needle), thread a length of either fishing line or fine horse hair. Thread the curved needle through one side of the muzzle to the other so that the needle curves backwards, causing the whiskers to do the same. Pull into place and trim.

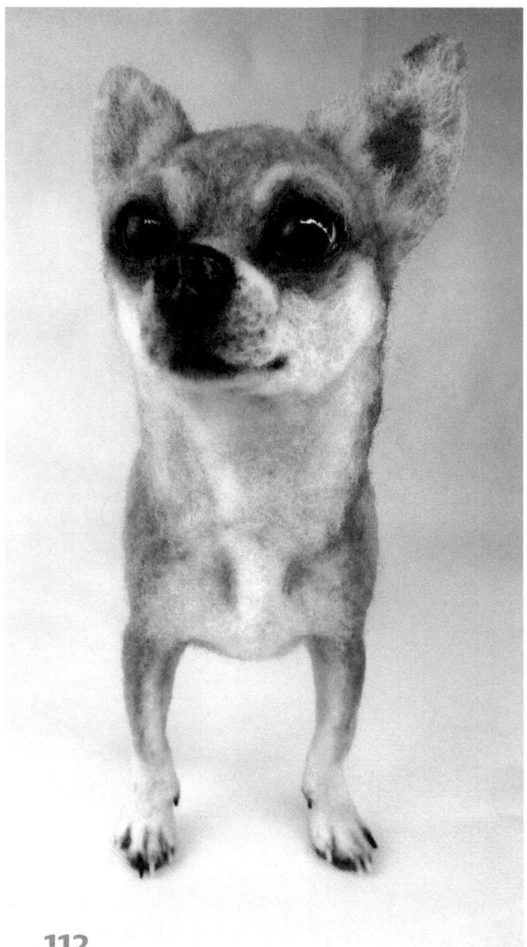

112

If you want to make the whiskers more secure, thread a longer length through the muzzle from one side to the other, tie a knot in the middle and pull the thread back through to the other side until the knot is caught inside the muzzle and locks in place.

Repeat for a further four or five whiskers

Give your Chihuahua one final check, adding finishing colour touches, and you're done!

THE DACHSHUND

This chapter will highlight a short coat, large ears and paws, a wax nose and out-of-proportion body.

A cabochon method of making eyes is also shown.

Study photos of black-and-tan Dachshunds to be sure of markings and shaping. Of course, you can make whatever colour Dachshund you want simply by changing the core wool colours to suit.

The creation and initial covering of the armature is not repeated in this and subsequent chapters as it is the same process for all the sculptures in this book, and is detailed in the Chihuahua chapter. Fine shaping and sculpting of detail is also left to personal artistic interpretation.

YOU WILL NEED

Materials

- Wire, 16-gauge, 1 x 36cm (14.14in) & 2 x 28cm (11.02in)
- Core (black), 100g (3.52oz) (World of Wool Carded Corriedale sliver, Raven)
- Core (tan), 50g (1.8oz) (The Felt Box No 22)
- Mid to dark grey Merino tops – any, 10g (0.35oz)
- 4 x 15.24cm (6in) glossy photo paper
- Eyes to print (brown)
- Flat-domed cabochons, 7mm (0.27in)
- Flat earring stud posts
- Felting wax, black
- Mod Podge, matt
- PVA glue
- Glossy Accents or Diamond Glaze
- Spectrum Noir pens: GB8, RB2, EB6, BG8, EB5, Black
- Silk Clay, black

Tools

- Wire cutters
- Pliers
- Tape measure/ruler
- Awl
- Scissors, small pointed
- Clay metal tools, small or dentist tools
- Tea-light, oil burner and candle
- Felting brush
- Multi-needle tool (sprung-type)
- Six large-headed pins
- Two small, round-headed pins
- 7mm (0.27in) paint brush

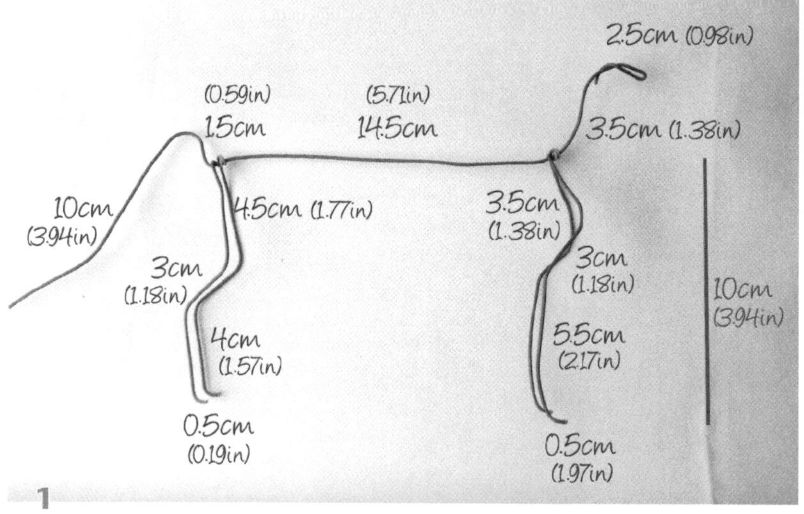

1

3

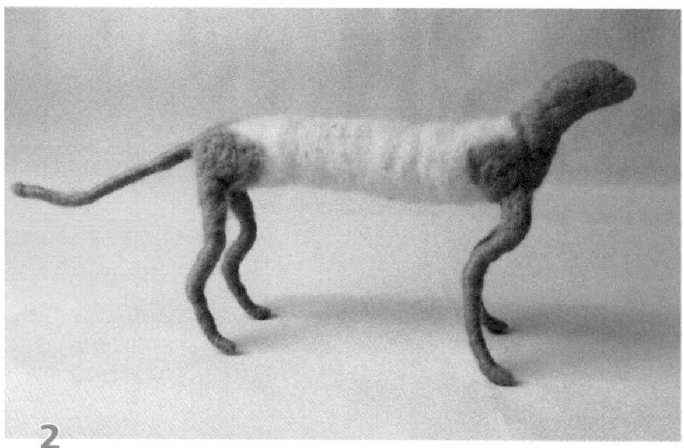
2

Step 1

1

Create an armature following the measurements of this plan and trim leg lengths once formed. Now pose your armature in the standing position, paying attention to the inward bent front legs and angular back legs.

Step 2
2, 3

Apply a basic covering of tan core wool and continue to make the basic shaping of the breed with this, using the same steps as in the Chihuahua chapter, making sure you then add bulk to the body in the same way, by adding lengths of wool to the sides and undersides of the body. Don't be tempted to continue to wrap your additions of wool to bulk the body as this will not create a good body shape.

NOTE: for the very first body/trunk wrapping you can use any core wool, as it will be covered by subsequent additions of wool.

Black-and tan breeds such as Dachshund, Doberman, Rottweiler, Toy Terriers, Manchester Terriers, Gordon Setters, some Spaniels, etc, all have the same black/tan pattern, so refer to breed photos showing this. Other black/tan breeds have a tan body and a black saddle, but, for the Dachshund, we are working on the bi-black/tan markings seen on the breeds mentioned.

Step 3
4-8

Build up the basic head shape, initially with tan core wool, remembering that the Dachshund has a very narrow, pointed muzzle and long head for the proportions of other body parts. Make the overall shaping of the paws, which are large for the breed's size, and create the characteristic, bent-in front legs that bow-out at the top, and the very angular hind legs. Ensure your sculpture will stand square unaided as you work.

The Dachshund's body is very low, the chest of some dogs almost touching the ground. Spend some time on the body and leg shaping, and keep assessing it from all

4

5

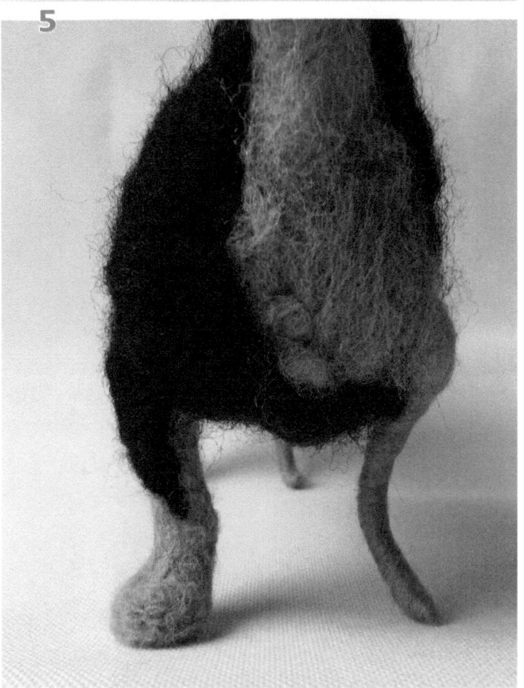

6

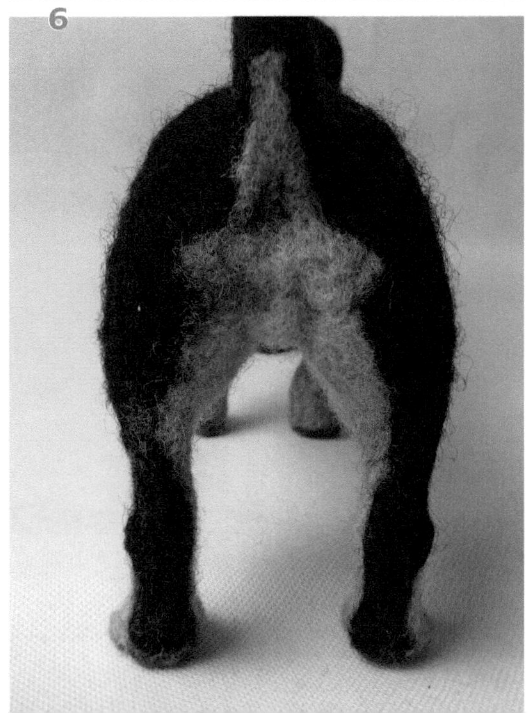

7

angles. When you have a fairly good overall shape, add some black core wool, following the coat pattern shown in the photos.

TIP

Sometimes it is helpful to take photos of your sculpture and also to look at it in a mirror, as this can show very obvious faults that your eye had become used to whilst working on it

Step 4

9, 10

Once you have a basic paw shape that is flat at the bottom, mark out where the pads will go. You can do this with a marker pen, or by adding the grey core freehand. Use some mid to dark grey tops for the pads. If you don't have the right grey, you can easily create this by blending 60/40 light grey/black Merino tops respectively. Hand-blended colours often look more

8

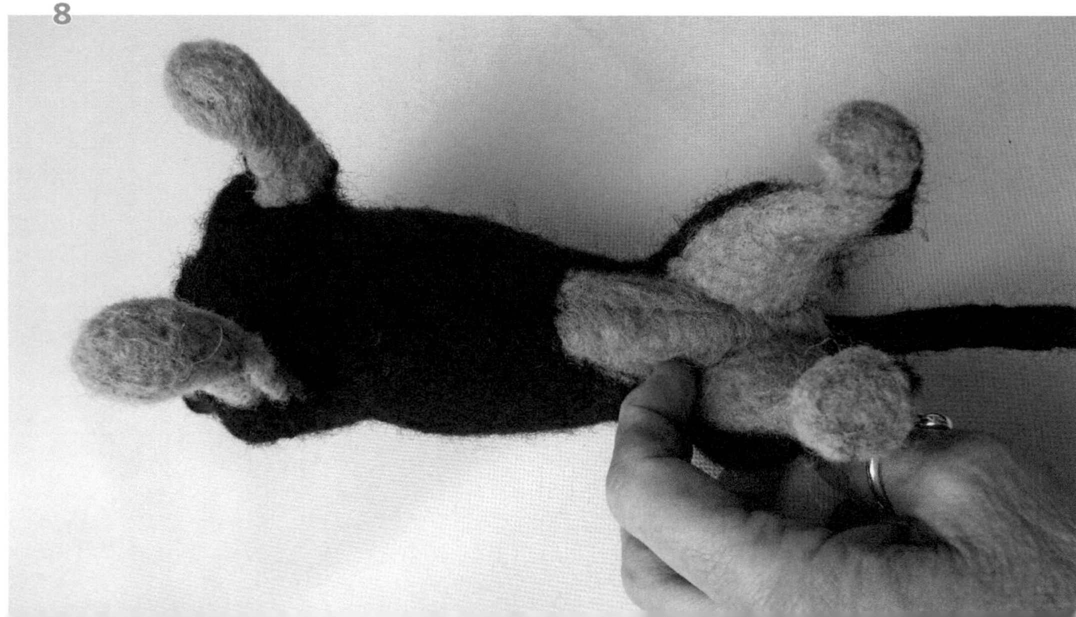

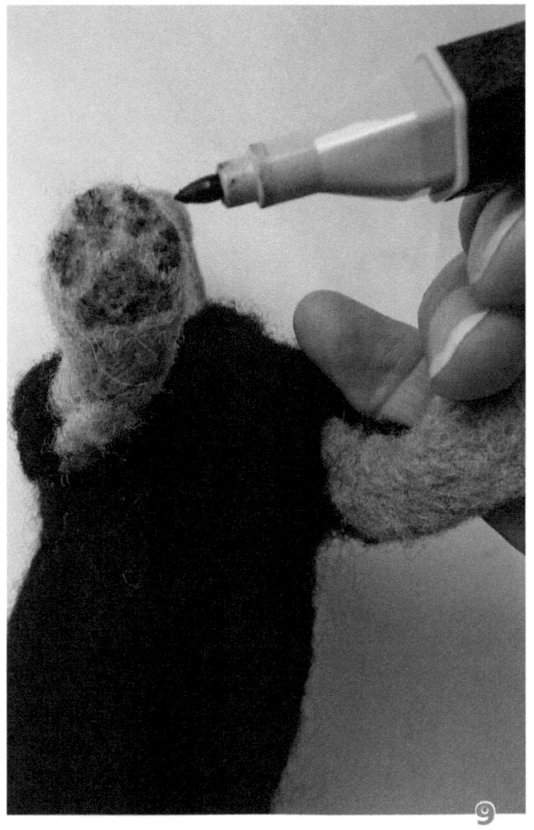

9

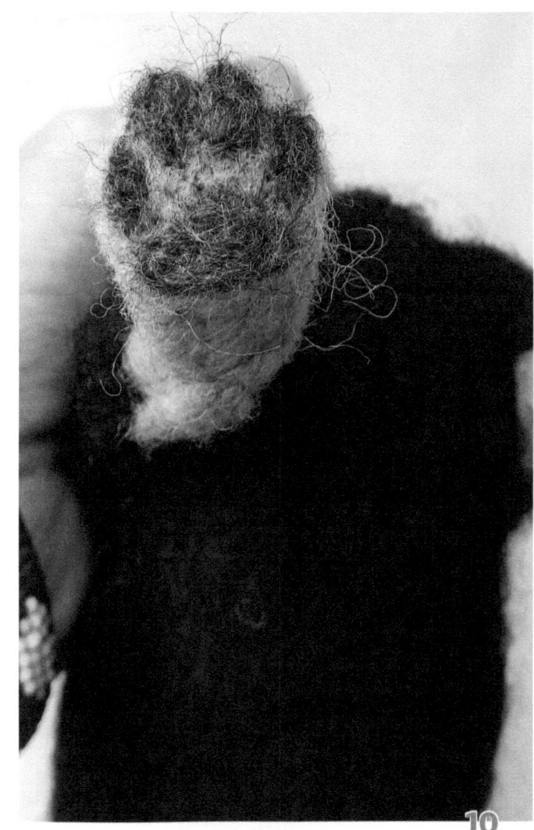

10

natural than straight dyed tops as they offer variations, and subtle tones of colour.

Add the pads in the same way as shown in the Chihuahua chapter, and don't forget the dewclaw pad at the back of the front legs. Dachshund paw pads are wider and slightly more splayed than those of the Chihuahua.

Step 5
11

As you add the pads, you might need to adjust the toes with more tan core to make them fit around the paw edges. When happy with the shaping of the paws, make three cuts into the paws to separate the toes (as you did with the Chihuahua paw). Be careful not to cut as far as the leg, but stop short of it.

As you make the cuts, be guided by the pads, cutting between them and with the cut in line with the body.

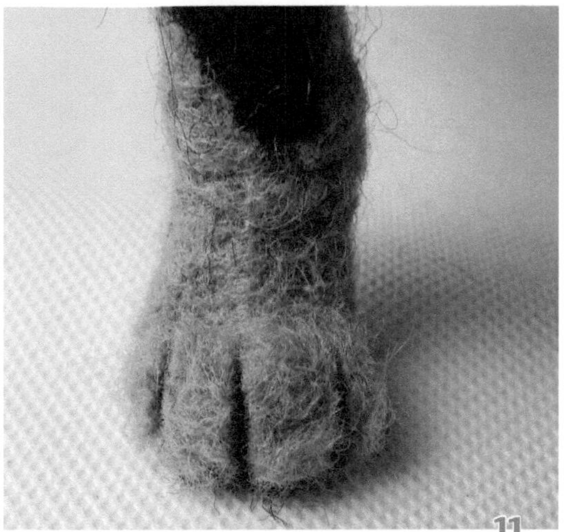

11

Step 6
12-14

Tidy the toes by felting down between them, trimming any sharp edges from any cuts made to the toes in the previous step, if needed. This defines and separates them. Pay attention also to the toe knuckle,

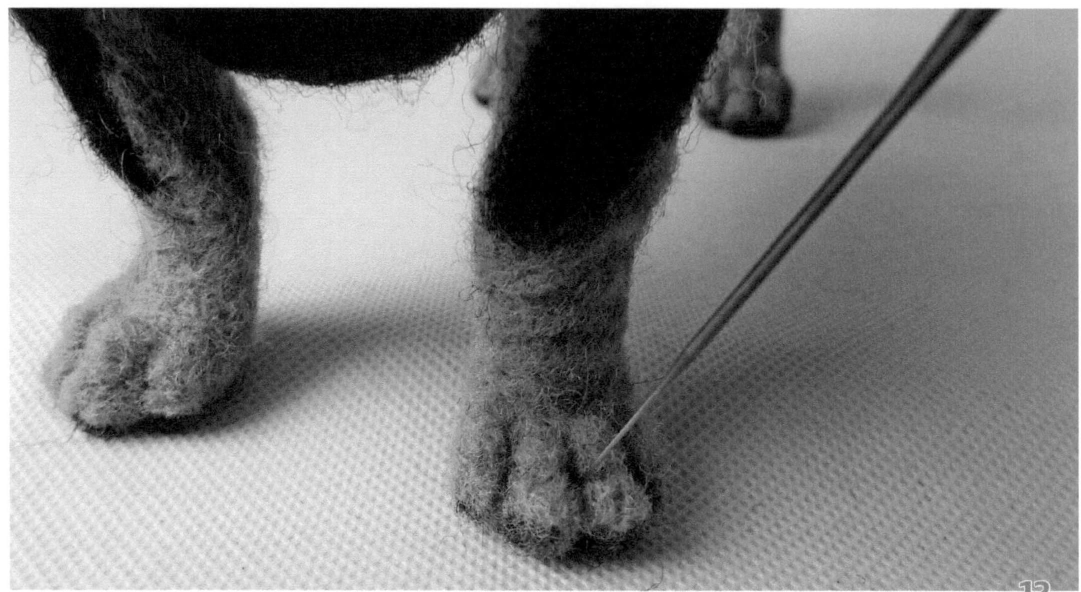

12

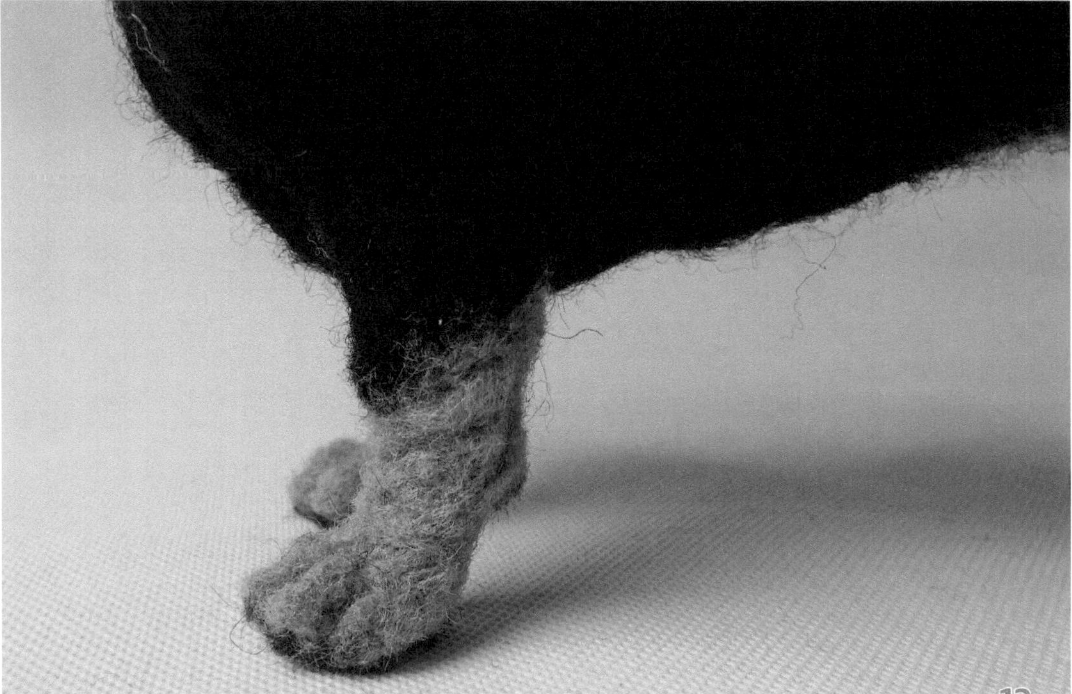

13

felting down the indents each side and adding a little more, if needed, to make the knuckles protrude. Felt the pads into the toes to give them a realistic look. This is a fiddly job and takes some time and patience. You can trim the toes into shape with scissors, too, if it helps, and can also add skin wrinkle detail on the legs by taking a small, fine length of tan core wool, and tacking one end to the inside of the leg, rolling it lightly, bringing it around the front of the leg and tacking it down on the other side. Felt down each side of the roll to achieve the wrinkle effect. Do the same for the back legs. Not all Dachshunds have these wrinkles, so you don't have to add them.

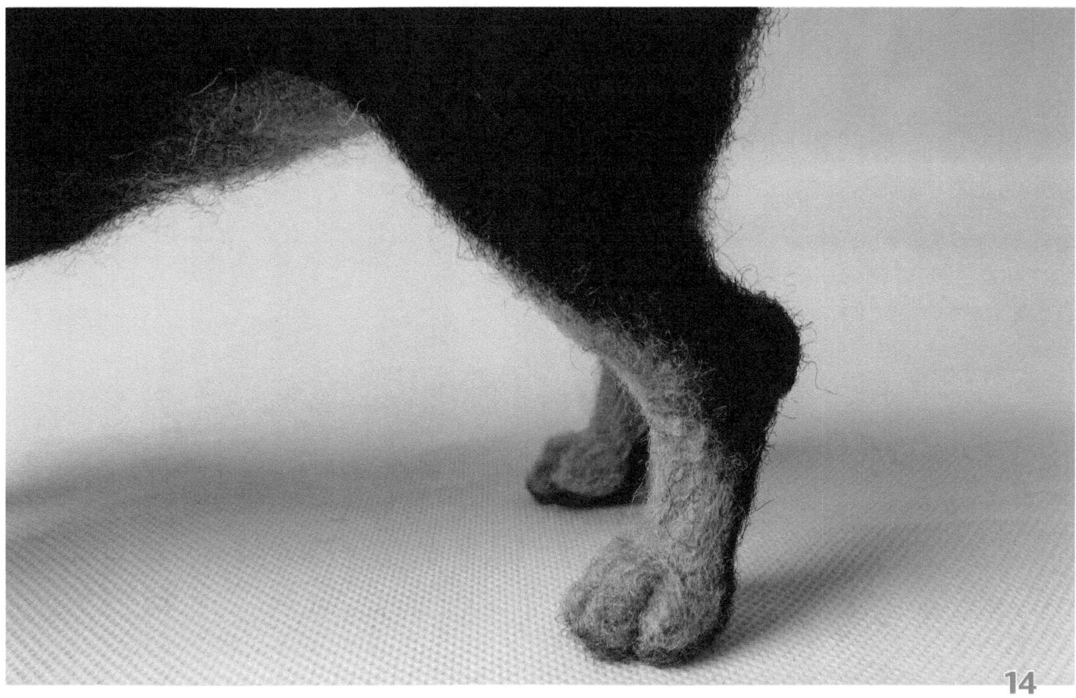

14

Step 7
15, 16

Now that you have a well-defined body shape that is quite firm to the touch (but, if not, build up the sculpture so that it is firmer to touch), start to blend along the edges of where the black meets the tan. Do this with a fine reverse needle, pushing into the shape in the opposite direction to hair growth, and slowly pulling it out in the direction of hair growth.

The aim is to pull out the tan wool from

15

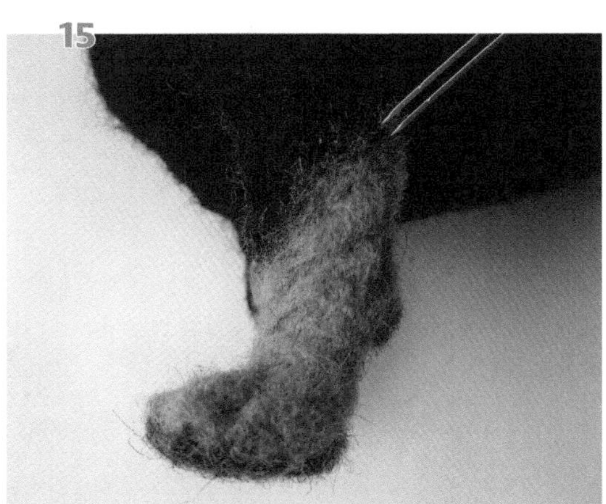

16

under the line of black wool, creating a gentle blend of both colours.

Trim away any fuzziness (don't be tempted to felt it back in as this will look messy). Reverse-felt a couple of tan triangles on the chest, or add a layer of tan wool to make them more pronounced, if you prefer. Dachshund markings vary greatly, and not all animals have well-defined tan triangles – some don't have any! – so decide which ones you would like to replicate. (Some very faint triangles were added to this sculpture at the end.) Trim when done.

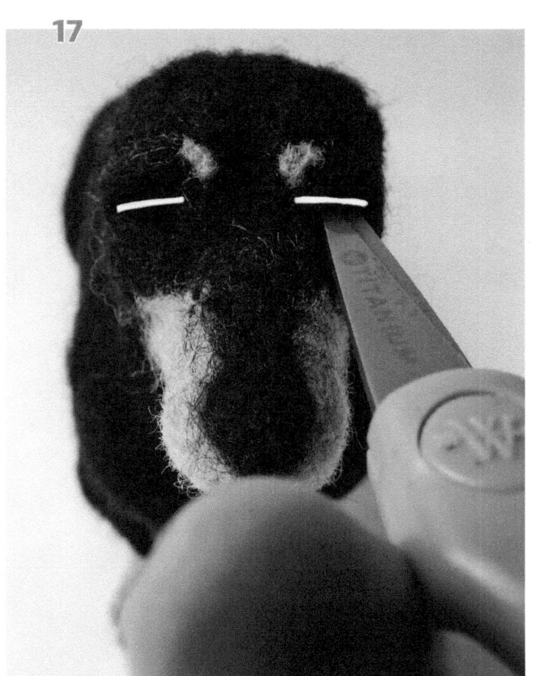
17

Step 8
17, 18

Add more shape to the head if needed, and make sure there is enough bulk to accommodate the eyes.

With a needle lightly mark out the mouth, then make a shallow cut, holding your scissors along the mouth but slanting downwards on the outer side, so that the cut is at an angle to create a more natural 'lip.' To mark out the eyes, felt rough horizontal lines where the eyes will go with a felting needle, shown by white lines. The eyes sit halfway between the end of the nose and the back of the head, and also level with the top line of the muzzle. Cut a 0.5cm (0.19in) deep horizontal hole, opening the hole with your scissors as you remove them from the cut.

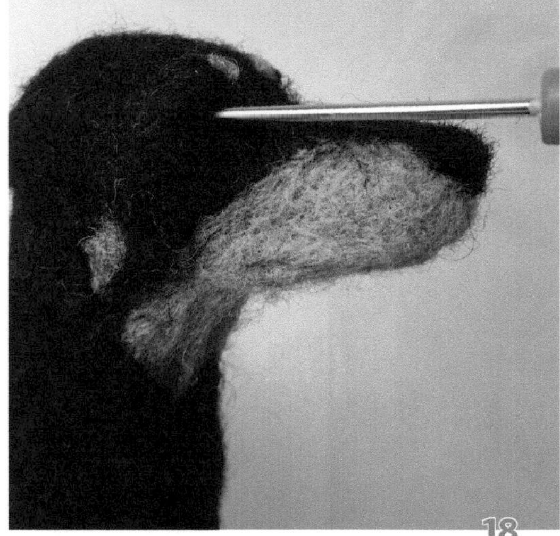
18

Step 9
19-22

To make the cabochon eyes, print out 7mm (0.27in) brown eyes onto glossy photographic paper (you can easily download nice eyes from the internet and print to size, or purchase printable ones from Etsy where all the sizing is done for you). You will need to intensify the eye-

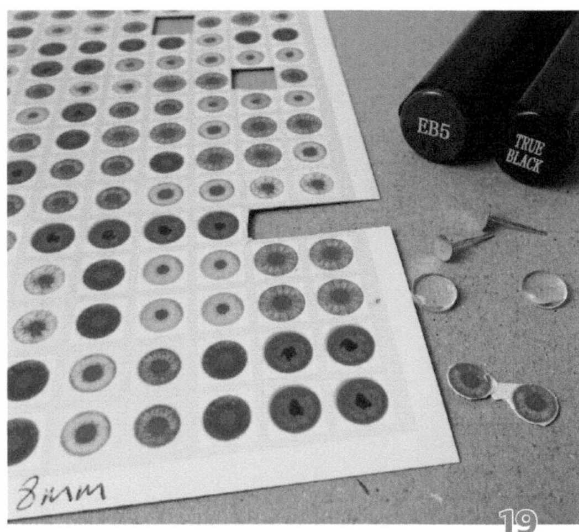

19

20

21

colour with Spectrum Noir pens; I used, EB5, GB8, and Black. Apply the colours gently and carefully and blur the pupil into the iris. You might want to print out a few pairs on which to practice first.

When you cut out the eyes, colour around the edge of the paper eye with pen EB5, or else it will show white. Then add a small drop of Glossy Accents or Diamond Glaze to the surface of each eye just coloured, and carefully place a 7mm (0.27in) cabochon on each, pressing down gently to expel any bubbles. Allow to cure.

Once cured, using a small amount of strong, quick-drying glue (superglue is perfect) attach a stalk to the back of each eye (this will make attaching the eye to the head a lot easier as the stalk helps to prevent the eye from moving about). Allow to dry. The end result should be beautiful brown eyes!

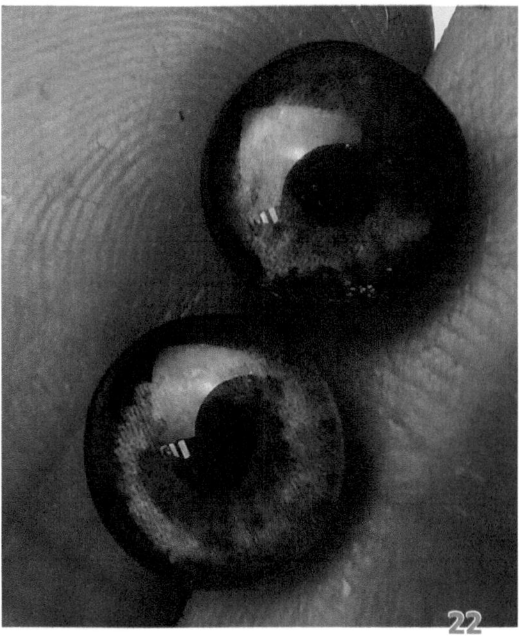

22

Step 10

23, 24

The cabochon eyes should now be ready to fit to the head. If you have felted the head rather tightly, decide where the eye will sit and poke the awl into the centre of each socket to help the eye stalks fit into the space. Make the hole as central

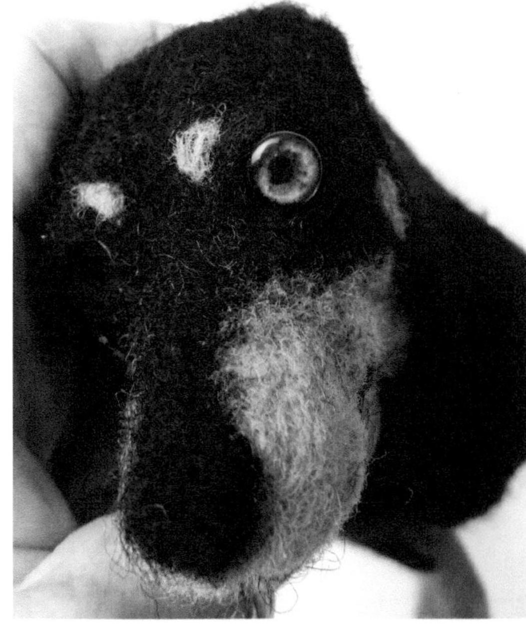

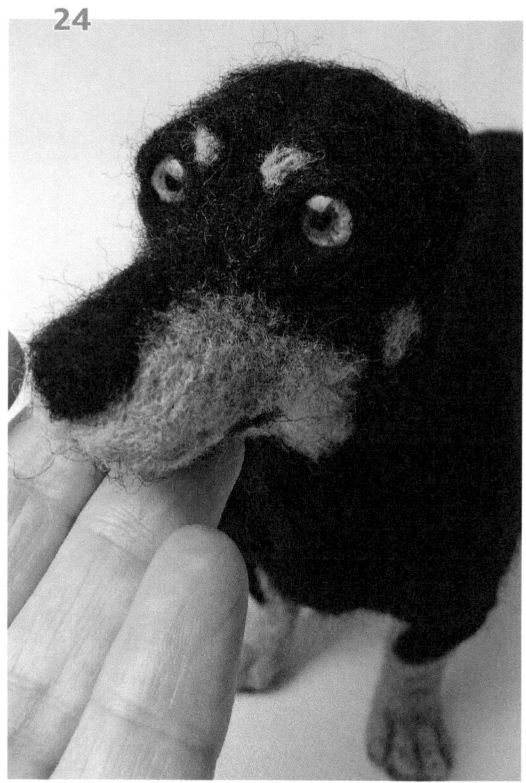

24

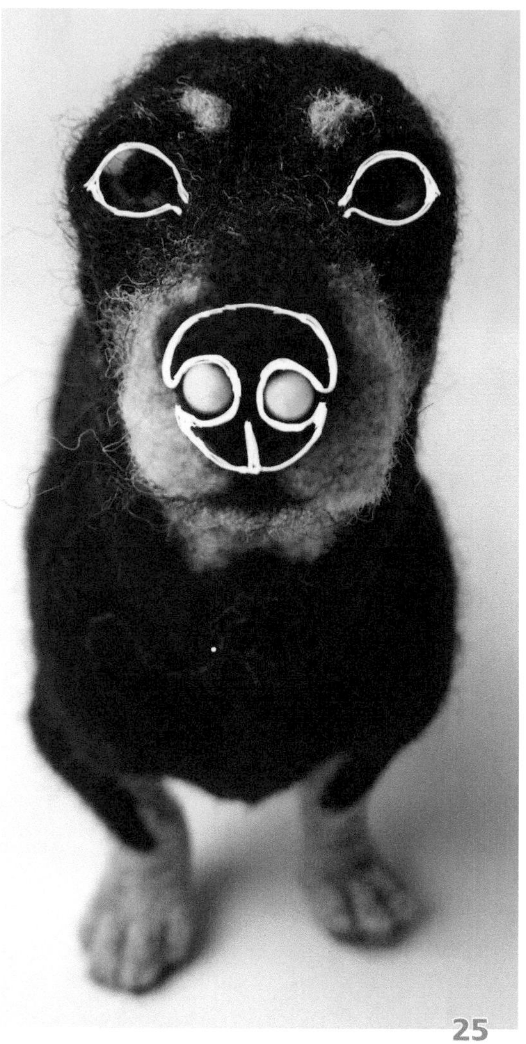

25

as possible and in-line with the head to ensure that the eyes sit level and look in the same/correct direction.

Once you have made a channel with the awl, offer up each eye stalk and slot into place. Use the awl to pull surrounding wool over the rim of the eyes to make them fit and sit correctly (his step usually takes quite a bit of fiddling to get right). Don't worry too much about the eye surround at this point, as we will build it up in the next step, but concentrate on getting the eyes level and looking in the same direction, and stay in place when you release them. You shouldn't need to glue them as the eyelids will hold them in place.

Step 11
25, 26

When you are happy with both eye locations, gently add small amounts of black core wool around the eyes, making the shape of the eyelids and building the eye surround on the head, paying attention to shape and size (rather almond-shaped: see white outline on image 25). You might find it helpful to hold the sculpture upside down when working on the eyes, but ensure both sides are equal, in any case.

With some back core wool, felt the basic shape of a nose, and place two round-headed pins where the nostrils will be. Ensure they are in line with each other (those in images 25 and 26 look a little lopsided!), and then begin to build up the nose around the pins (the pins help to create a more detailed shape).

The Dachshund nose is very pointed,

26

and extends over the end of the muzzle. When you have felted the nose so that it is as hard as possible, carefully remove the pins and felt inside the nostrils: you might find it helpful to use some very small, pointed scissors to trim where needed to create the right shape. Take care you don't felt the nose flat, and use the awl to gently pull out into shape parts any you may have flattened.

Make a cut each side of each nostril (see white outline on image 25) to define the side nose openings.

Felt in the edges of these to make a clear divide, as per canine noses.

Step 12
27, 28

Now give the nose a good surface trim to get rid of any fuzziness, and then a coat of Mod Podge Matt to make a hard surface on which to place the felting wax, to prevent it soaking into the wool. Allow to dry. Next, heat a small amount (about one teaspoon) of black felting wax, using your ceramic oil/tea-light burner and, with a small metal flat modelling/dental tool with a 3mm (0.11in) end, apply the wax to the nose by dipping the end of the tool into the melted wax, and applying the wax to the nose, little by little, and staying within the nose boundary lines. Don't allow the wax to run onto the muzzle. Now and then you may need to wipe or scrape away residual wax on the tool.

27

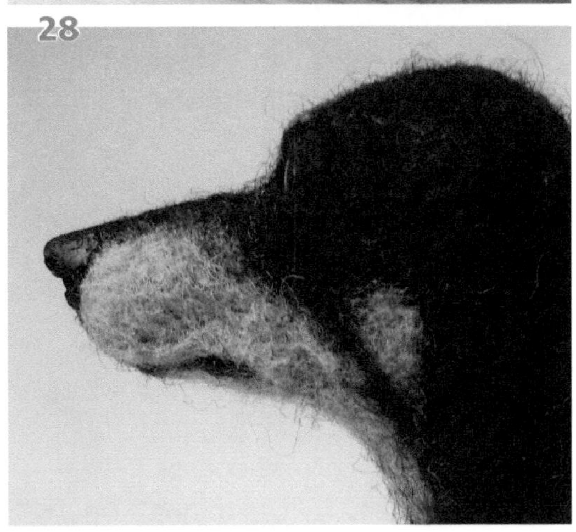
28

Once you have a good nose covering, you'll notice it is messy in appearance. To rectify this clean the metal tool as described above, then hold it in the candle flame for a few seconds to warm, then re-mould, smooth and fashion the wax on the nose (this will take some practice to get right). You may need to add more wax.

Whilst the wax is warm, you can also texture and mould it with your fingers. The finished nose can also be gently sanded to a smooth but textured finish using a piece of medium sandpaper, or one of those sanding sponge blocks found in Pound Shops.

TIP

If the metal tool gets too hot, it will immediately melt the wax, causing it to drip/run, and even burn and so lose shape. Getting the right length of time over the flame will take some practice. You will also need to regularly clean the metal tool, especially if working with clear or light-coloured wax, as the soot will colour the wax

If planning on using this method often, heat the wax inside an empty tea-light holder, which can be placed on top of the ceramic saucer, keeping it free of wax, obviating the need to empty and clean this if changing wax colours

Step 13

29

Add a very fine line of grey Merino tops (the same as used for the pads) to the inside of the eyes to make eyelids, which need to be very fine (a fiddly job). Add more to the inside corner of each eye, and be sure to make a good angle on the outside corner of each eye. Trim when done.

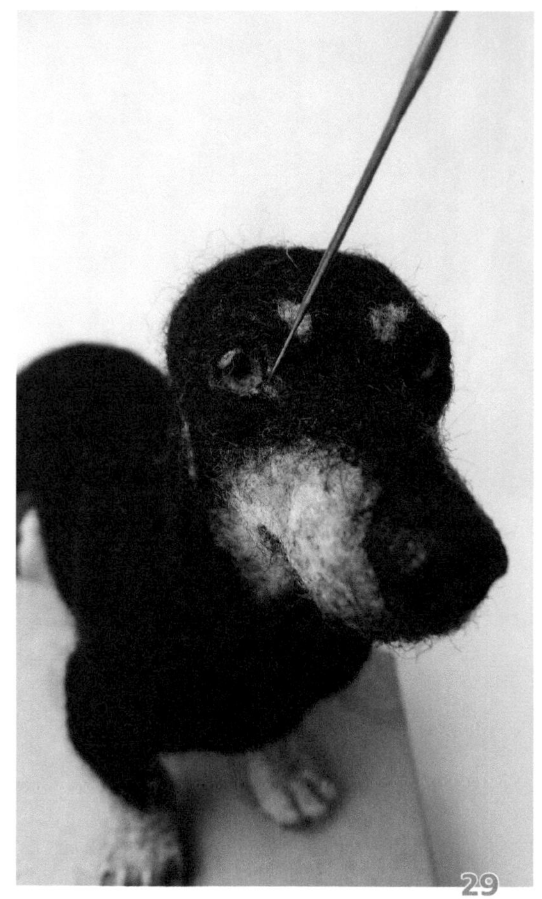

29

Step 14

30, 31

To add colour detail to the tan core wool, first add black toe markings along the ridges of each toe with a Spectrum Noir black pen. Lightly run a BG6 pen in-between the toes to give a little more definition and depth. Where you have reverse-felted between the black and tan core, where the tan begins, lightly colour with pen GB8 to give a little darker definition. If you inadvertently colour too much, cover and tone down with tan core.

Mark out the mouth detail with a black pen, and add the whisker spots very carefully with the pointed end: use GB8

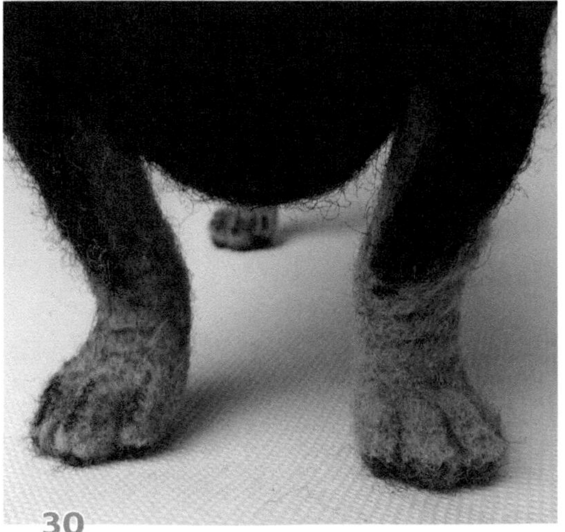

30

31

on the edge of the tan and EB6 and BG6 around the muzzle.

Step 15

32

To make the ears, using a felting brush, an awl, and a multi-needle tool (the sprung type), create a flat ear shape using the ear template. Lay black core wool in fine amounts onto the felting brush in a rough approximation of the ear shape, and felt down using the multi-needle tool. Using the awl, carefully lift the ear off the felting brush so that you don't stretch it out of shape. Felt both sides, alternating between them equally, until you have a nicely felted ear shape that isn't see-through when held up to the light, but also not too thick. Reinforce with more black core wool if needed.

To tidy the edges, either trim with scissors, or work around the edge felting

32

inwards or along the edge using a fine needle, holding the ear between thumb and forefinger as you work. You need only tidy the exposed edges, leaving fuzzy that part that will attach the ear to the head. Place the ears back-to-back and trim to the same size and shape.

Step 16
33-35

To attach the ears, first ensure they are the correct way around for each side of the head: the straighter edge is the front of the ear. Hold the ear in position as shown, so that the front of the ear with the straight edge is facing forward, and the more curved part of the ear is facing backward.

33

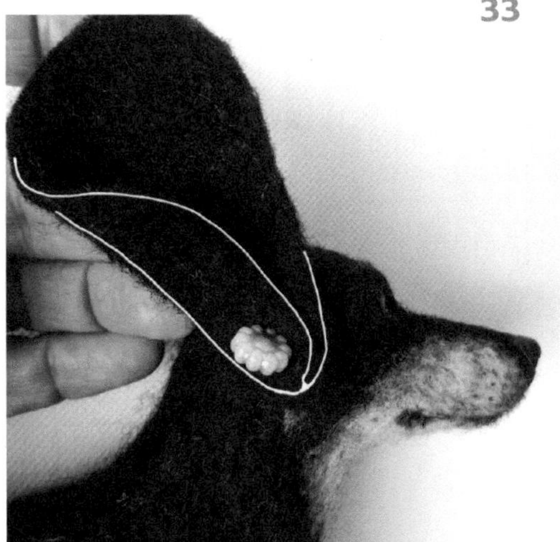

34

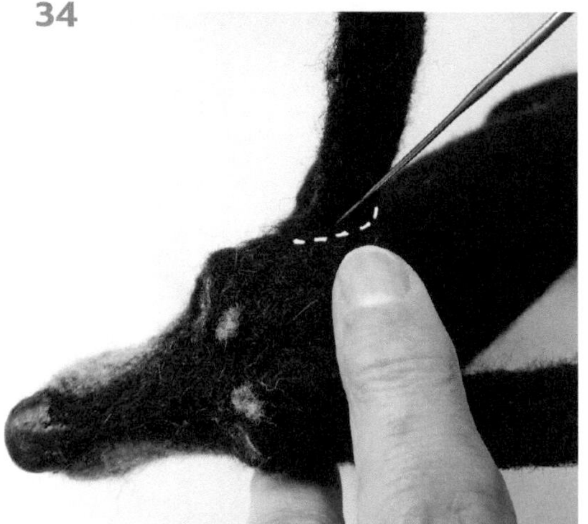

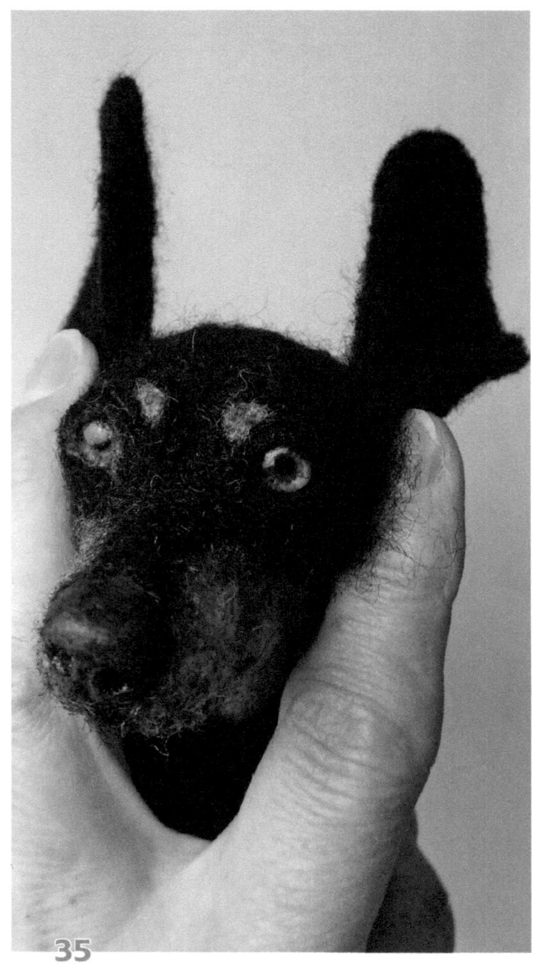

35

Take the curved part (facing backward) and fold it over the bottom half of the ear, as shown by the white lines in the photo Secure with a large-headed pin. Felt down from the inside of the ear to attach it to the head. Do the same to the other side, making sure both ears are of equal length before pinning the other side– check this by holding them upright to meet over the head.

With both ears roughly attached, fold down into final position and pin in place, so that you can now felt around the back and top of the ears, adding a little more black core wool over the joins to secure them in place, and blend them seamlessly into the head. Felt inside and outside the ears. Remove the pins when done.

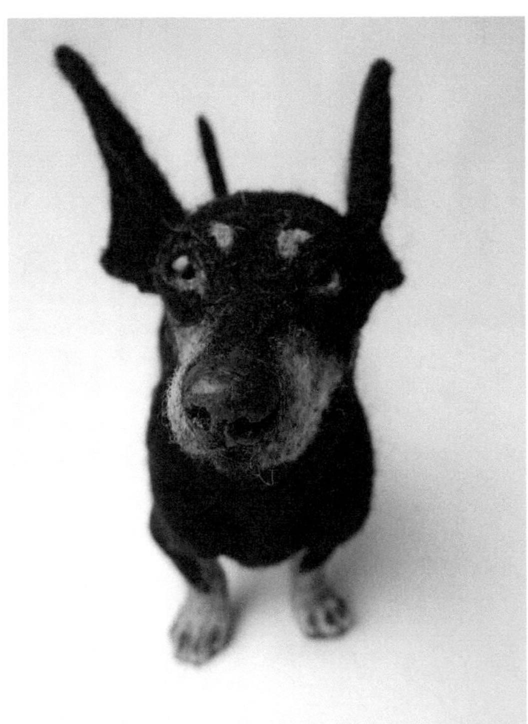

36

Step 17
36-38

It's possible that the ears may not stay in place. To rectify this, either felt them into place against the neck, or apply a thin layer of Mod Podge on the upper inside bent part of the ear, holding in position with a pin until dry.

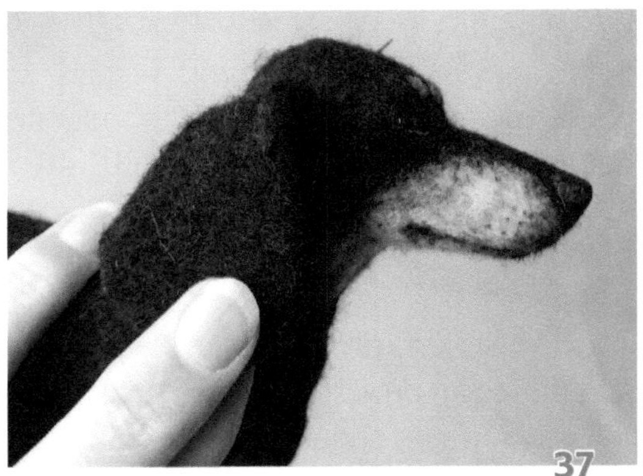

37

38

Step 18

A coat of Mod Podge Matt will make the paw pads more realistic, but the pads must be firmly felted and the surfaces trimmed, or else the Mod Podge will not give a good coating. Felt inwards around the edges of each pad to tidy the shaping, adding more grey tops if needed. Give the pads a surface trim and apply a thin coat of Mod Podge Matt to the pads only. Allow to dry, then gently reverse-felt around the pad edges and in-between the toes to simulate natural hair.

Step 19

39-41

The Dachshund has very distinctive nails, and these can be achieved by rolling black Silk Clay into nail shapes. Begin by rolling a small amount of clay to around 2mm (0.07in) thickness, and cut into 36 lengths of 5-6mm (0.19-0.23in). Gently roll one end thinner to taper to a blunt-ended nail. and introduce a slight bend in the nail. Let them cure for about 20 minutes. 18 nails of various sizes are needed: larger ones for the middle toes and smaller ones for the outside toes (4 x 4 paws = 16 plus 2 dewclaws = 18). Always make twice as many as you need as this will give a good choice of nails, and will also prove useful for future projects.

When the nails have set, fit them using the same method as given in the Chihuahua chapter. You may need to add a little extra tan core wool around some of the nails to make them look correct on the paw; this will depend on how accurate the paws are.

Step 20

42

Create a little carpal pad on the back of each front leg. Dachshund dewclaws

39

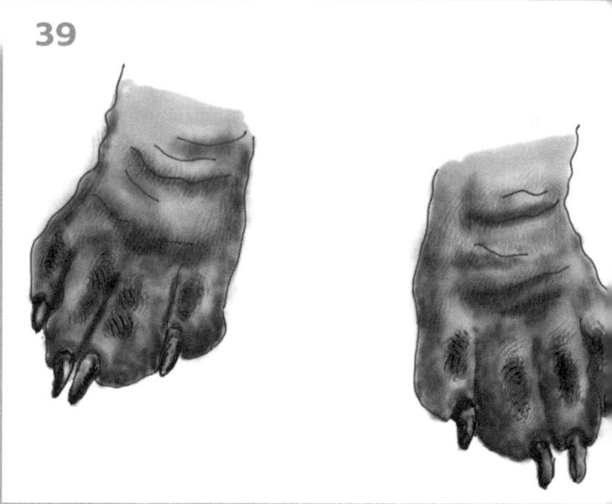

40

41

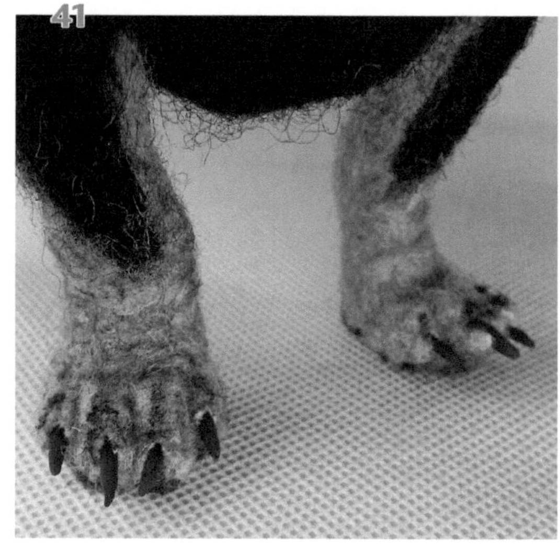

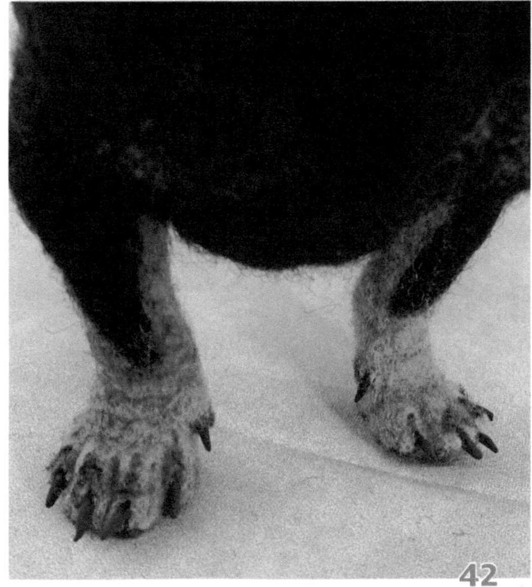

are sited slightly lower than many other breeds; just below the pastern joint. Felt on a small amount of tan core wool, then add some grey Merino tops for the pad. Cut a slit for the dew claw to be glued in the same way as the rest. Give each nail a thin coating of Mod Podge Matt to disguise the dull finish of the Silk Clay.

Step 21

All that's left to do now is touch up any markings with the alcohol pens, as necessary, and you're done!

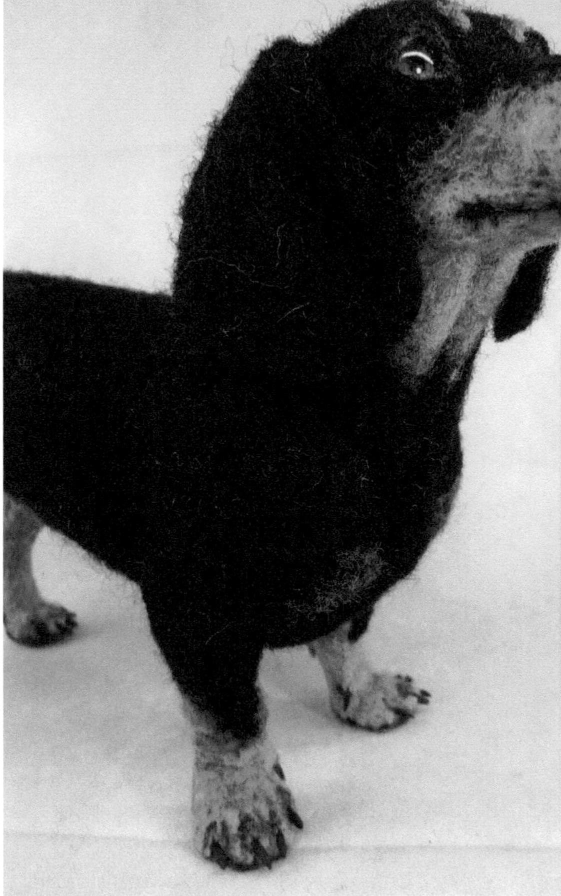

THE YORKSHIRE TERRIER

This chapter will show you how to add long fur (Merino tops) attachments, blending, highlighting of fur, clipping, texturing, and other finishing touches.

The instructions for detailed nose shaping and how to create paws are not repeated in this chapter as they are the same as described in the chapter covering the Chihuahua (though without nails in the case of the paws).

YOU WILL NEED

Materials

- Wire, 16-gauge, 1 x 38cm (14.96in) & 2 x 30cm (11.8in)
- Core (tan), 80g (2.82oz) (The Felt Box No 22)
- Core (black), 50g (1.7oz) (World of Wool Carded Merino Batt Raven)
- Core (pink), 10g (0.35oz) (World of Wool Carded Corriedale sliver, Candy Floss)
- Tops (cream), 30g (1.05oz) (World of Wool Merino Tops Oyster or Sandstone)
- Tops (fawn), 30g (1.05oz) (Adelaide Walker Merino Tops Sand)
- Tops (black), 30g (1.05oz) (World of Wool Merino Tops Raven)
- Tops (grey), 40g (1.14oz) (World of Wool Merino Tops Granite)
- Tops (tan), 40g (1.41oz) (World of Wool Merino Tops Antique)
- Acrylic off-white beads 2 x 10mm (0.39in) plus 2 x 10mm (0.39in) spacer beads, any colour
- Silk Clay, black
- Diamond Glaze
- PVA glue
- Mod Podge Gloss
- Spectrum Noir pens: EB3, EB8 and True Black
- L'Oreal Elnett Satin aerosol-free, pump-action hairspray, or similar

Tools

- Felting sponge/mat
- Wire cutters
- Plyers
- Awl
- Tape measure/ruler
- Scissors, small pointed, and a pair of larger ones for cutting the tops
- Felting brush
- 3-needle tool (sprung-type)
- 3-needle tool/quad needle (open-type

to make faster work of base shaping)
- Pair of mini, metal-toothed hand carders (metal dog brushes work just as well)
- 8mm (0.31in) circle template
- Small, rubber-tipped clay tools: one pointed and one horseshoe-shaped
- Nail file, or something similar
- Fine (nail art-type) brush, and a larger, softer one
- Three large-headed pins
- Two small, round-headed pins

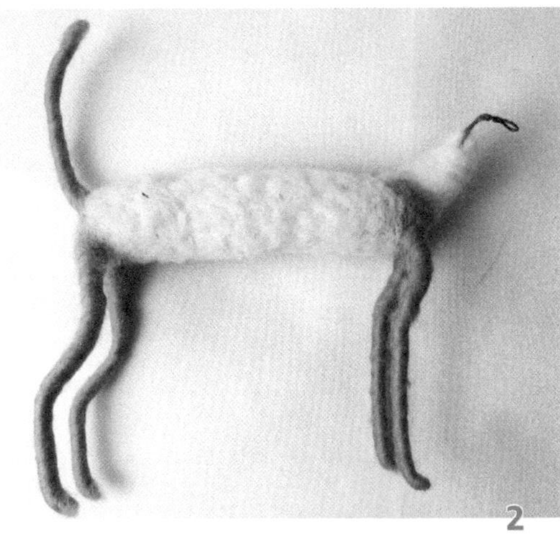

2

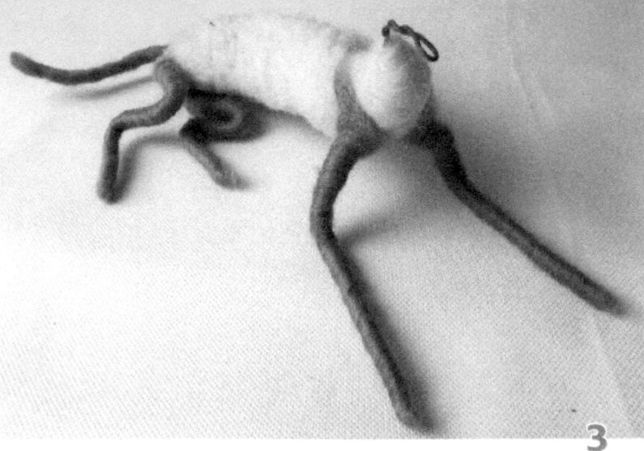

3

Step 1
1-3

Create the armature using the measurements given in (1), and form the legs, then trim these to length. With the armature in the standing position, apply the first complete base covering of core tan wool, using the method described in the Chihuahua chapter.

Once everything is covered, pose your Yorkie in the down position (you might have to fiddle about with this as the sculpture must be able to lay on a flat surface completely unaided). It sometimes helps to bend the wire armature a little further than you need to, to get the limbs to stay where you want them. The important thing to remember is not to continue adding more wool to an armature that isn't in the correct position to start with, as mistakes of this kind can be very difficult to rectify later. Much more wool will subsequently be added to the body, so make allowance for this when forming the pose. For example, the trunk of the sculpture should not touch the surface at this stage.

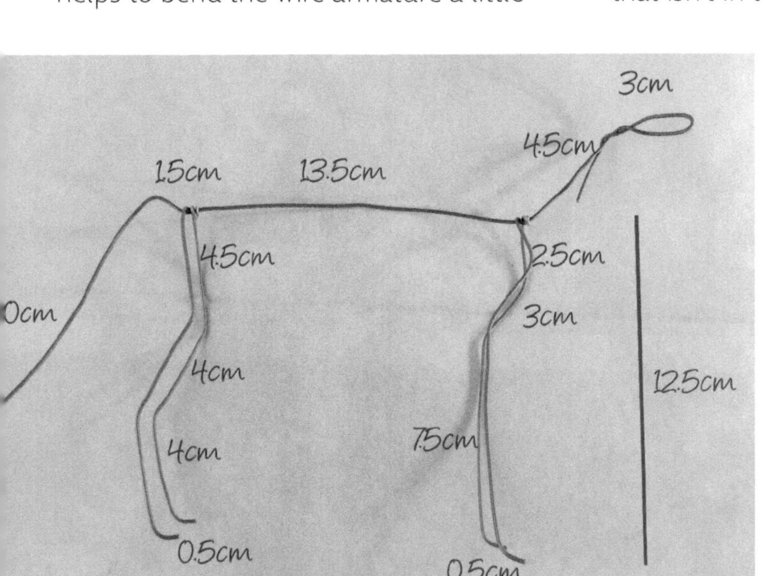

1

Step 2
4-8

Begin building up the shape and form of your Yorkie with the tan core wool, constantly

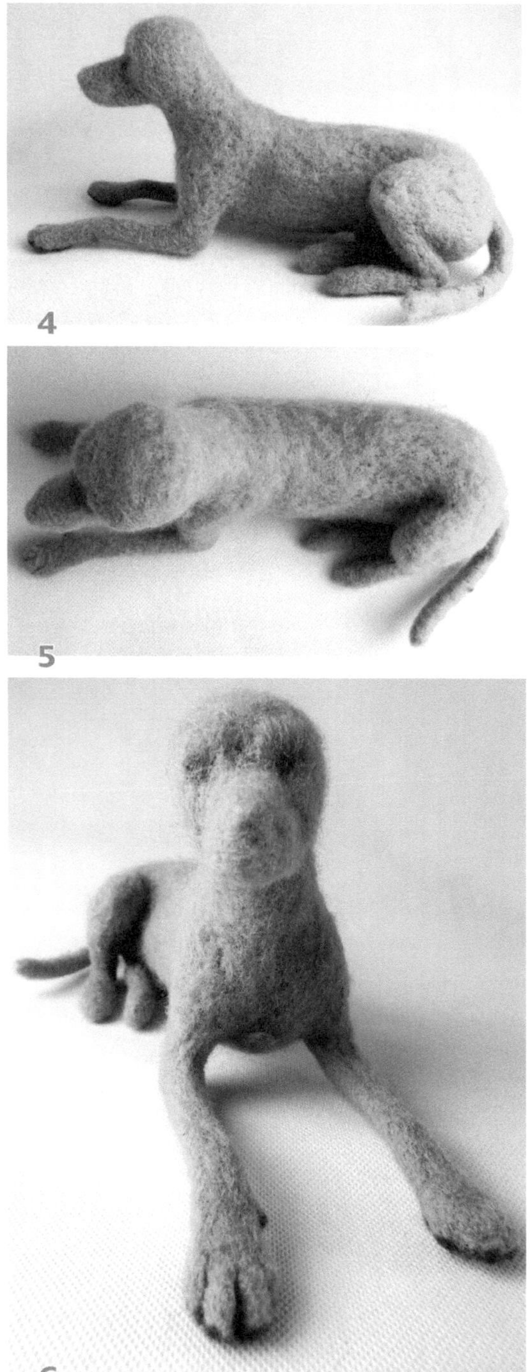

4

5

6

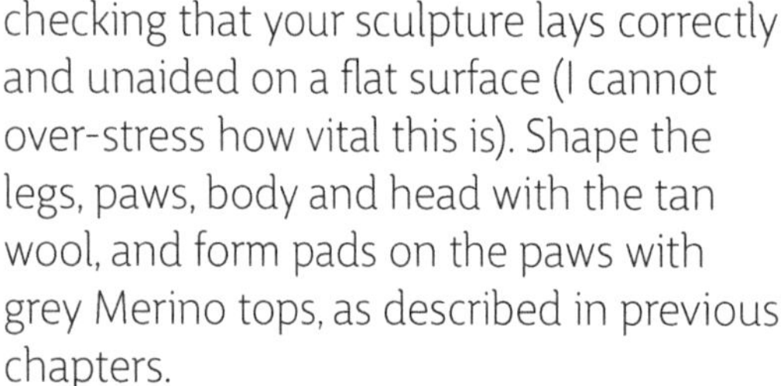

checking that your sculpture lays correctly and unaided on a flat surface (I cannot over-stress how vital this is). Shape the legs, paws, body and head with the tan wool, and form pads on the paws with grey Merino tops, as described in previous chapters.

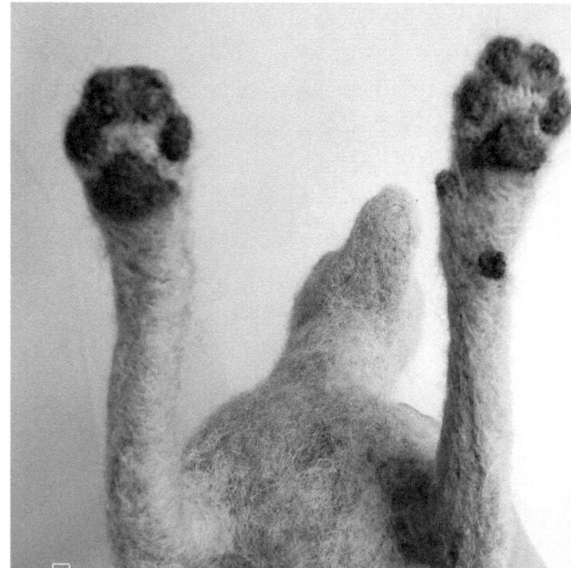

7

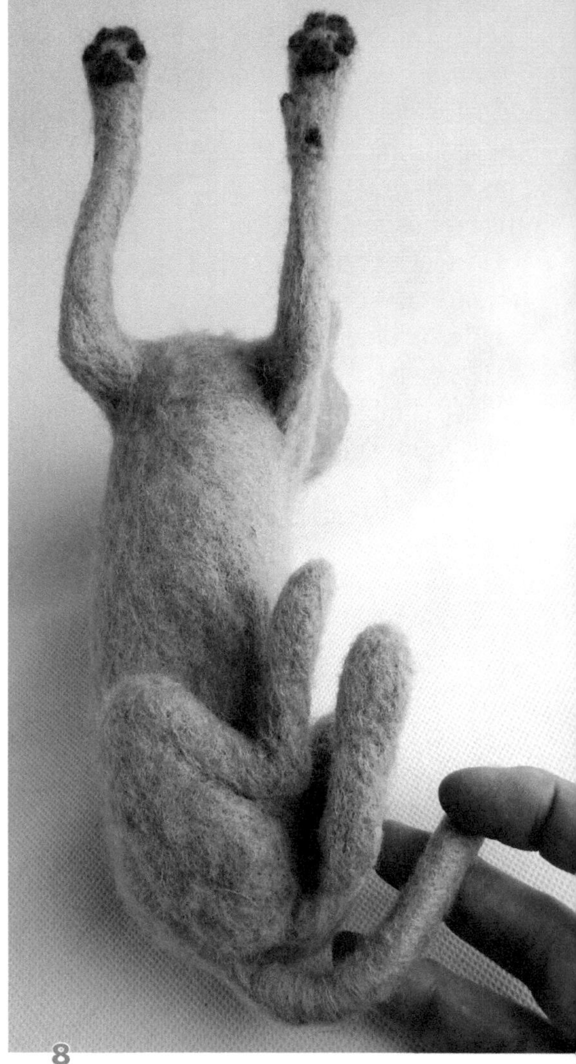

8

TIP

Although perfect detail on the legs, body and face might not strictly be needed for this sculpture, as it is being completely covered in long fur, from which you can also create form and shaping, it is good practice to add as much detail as you can to the base body shaping, as this WILL shine through in the final touches. It also helps hone your skills so that you improve with every creation. I encourage you to Google photos of 'shaved Yorkies' to better see their body shaping and details

Step 3

9, 10

Using the Chihuahua chapter for detailed instruction, mark where the eyes will be positioned, either by felting an indent, or marking with an alcohol pen (as if the dogs eyes are closed), before making any cut. These marks should be no wider than 9mm (0.35in) as the beads are 10mm (0.39in), and need to fit snugly within the socket. The bottom eyelid should sit just below the top line of the muzzle in each case, so that the eyeline is level with the top of the muzzle. At this point you may realise that there isn't enough bulk

9

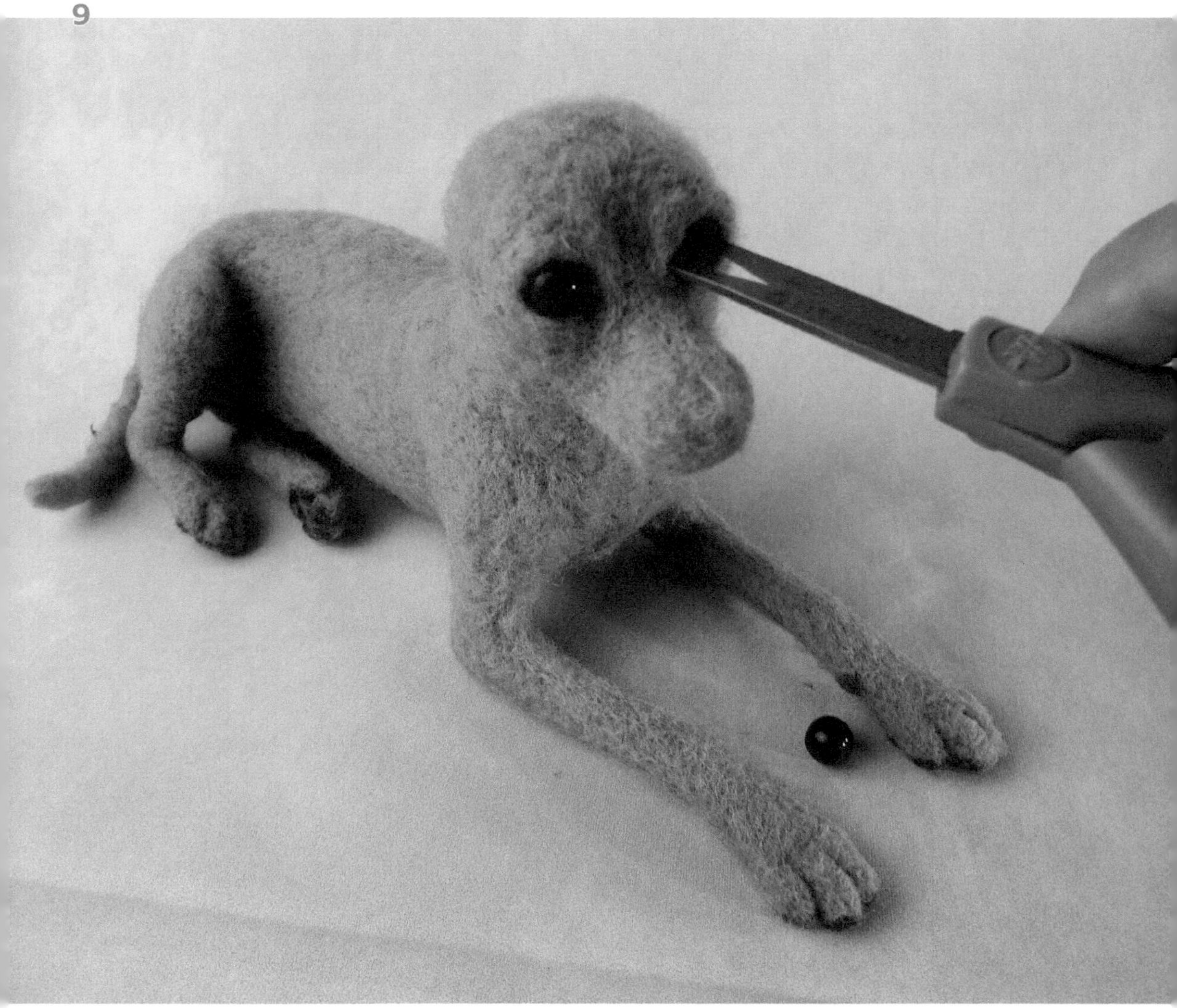

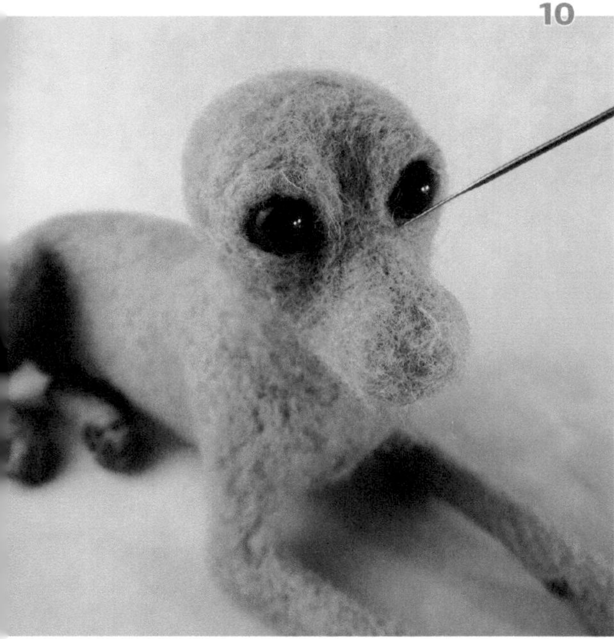
10

on the head or around the eyes, so add accordingly.

Make a couple of horizontal cuts of 9mm (0.35in) wide and at least 9mm (0.35in) deep, then open up the cavity with the scissors, twisting these a little as you remove them from the cut. This should be fairly easy to do as long as the head has not been felted too tightly.

With the awl, coax each spacer bead into position, and hold in place with your thumb whilst using the awl to pull the 'eyelids' (top of the cut) over the beads. This may take a few attempts to get the beads to stay in place in the same position and protruding by the same amount. You might need to add a little more core wool around the eyes to give them more shape and detailing, but remember that the eye openings will need to be a little wider than the finished item, around 1mm (0.039in) wider, as you will be adding Silk Clay eyelids, which will make the eye openings slightly smaller.

Aim to have a little under half of the spacer bead visible, with the remaining covered. The eye sockets will be right when it's possible to insert and remove the beads without having to make any adjustment, and they sit perfectly in place; the aim, of course, being to create perfectly-shaped sockets, into which the handcrafted eyes can be easily inserted without damaging them.

Step 5
11-13

The next stage is to make the eyes. Use a pair of 10mm (0.39in) off-white acrylic beads and, with the 8mm (0.31in) circle template, colour inside the circle with the EB8 pen in a clean, circular movement, working from the outside in, as described in the Chihuahua chapter. Leave to dry, then dab on the pupil with the true black pen, making a mottled line of colouring between the brown and black. Don't overdo it at this stage or you may spoil the colouring already done. Leave to dry.

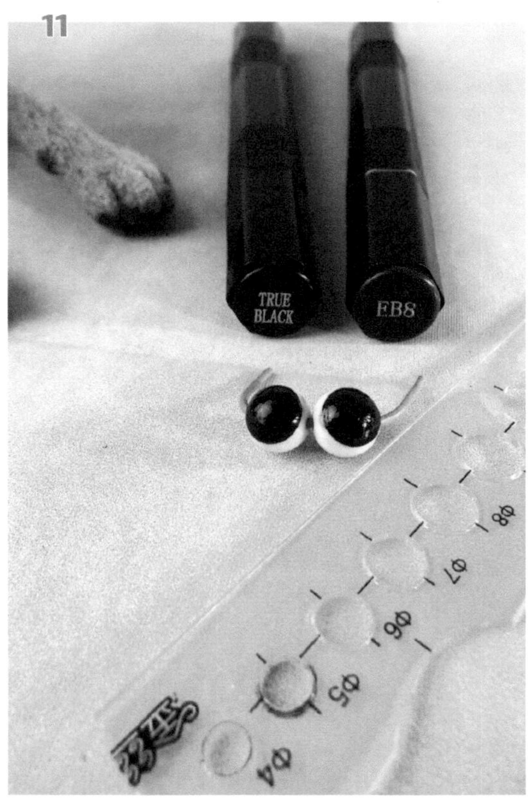

11

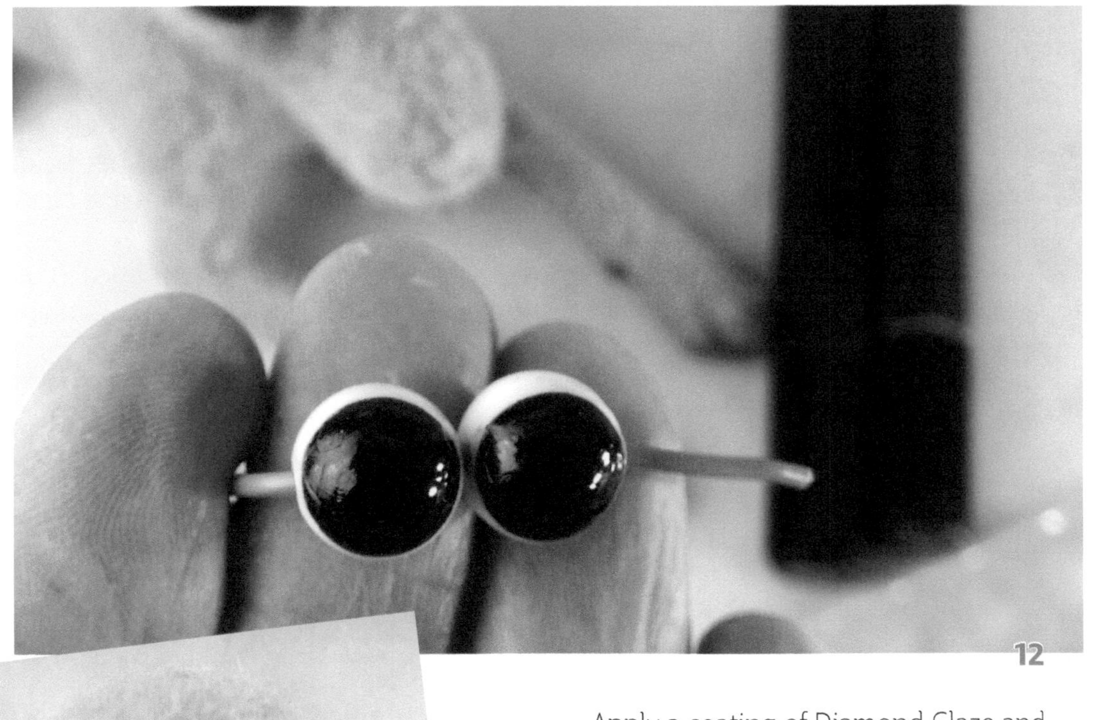

12

Apply a coating of Diamond Glaze and allow to dry. Fine-tune your colouring over the glaze by dabbing the brown around the edge of the iris to give it definition, and also blend the colouring between the pupil and the iris with the brown and black pens. Give another coat of glaze and leave to dry. Fit the eyes to see how they look, and to check that the eye sockets are the correct size. Remove and replace with the spacer beads.

Step 6
14-17

To make the ears cut Antique Merino tops into 2.5cm (0.98in) lengths and brush with the carders to separate the fibres and make them fluffy and easier to felt (described in the Blending chapter). Place enough on the felting brush to make a triangle about 5cm (1.96in) long, with a little extra at the bottom to use for attachment, and 5.5cm (2.16in) wide at the base. (Yorkie ears are quite long and pointed.) Felt down the triangle shape (but not the extra allowance), periodically lifting

13

the ear off the brush with the awl, turning it over and felting down the other side, adding more wool as needed so that the ear is thin, but not see-through when held up to the light. Make two of the same size and thickness.

You might like to add another hue to the Antique Merino by blending it with Granite Merino in the ratio of 4:2, but add this colour only to the back of each ear, so that the colouring is deeper on the outside. To help prevent colours mixing too much, felt

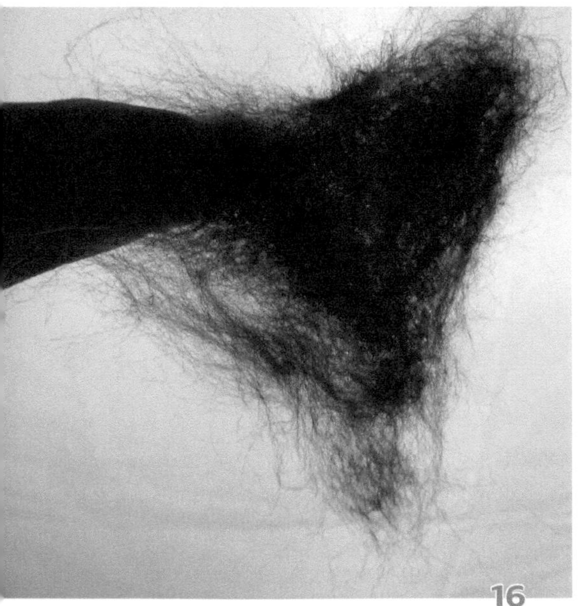
16

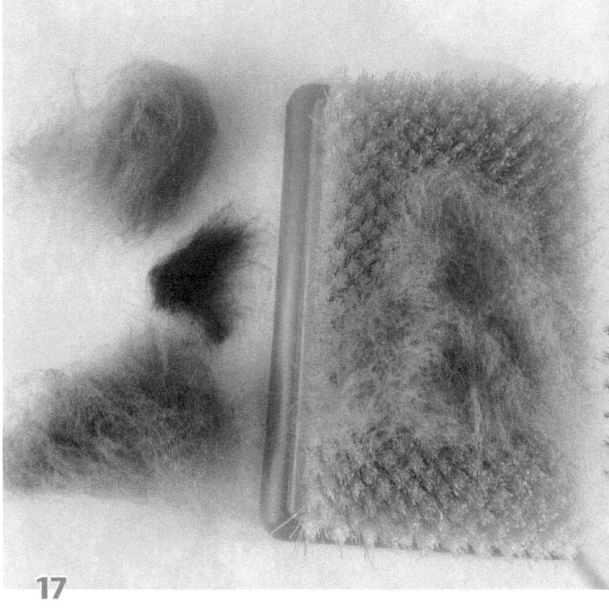
17

in the darker colour with the sprung multi-needle tool, on the dark side only and felt gently (try not to felt right through the ear; simply let the needles catch the surface).

When you have a good uniform triangle shape, use a single needle to tidy along the two top edges of each ear. Felt in any stray wool to make a nice straight edge, leaving the bottom edge fuzzy. Trim both ears along the two top edges and on both surfaces, and place back-to-back to check they are the same size and shape. Trim as needed.

TIP

Before you locate the ears, ensure that the back of the head is not too rounded, or else the ears will not sit correctly in position on each side, slightly proud of the back of the head

Step 7
18-22

With the correct head shaping ready for the ears, use three large-headed pins to hold them in place: one each side of

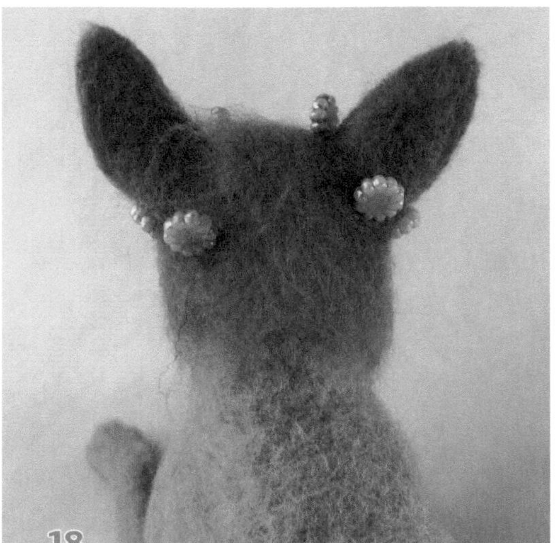
18

19

the ear, and one at the back. It may be necessary to re-pin them a couple of times to get them sitting correctly, and are equal and the same height. Don't worry about the excess at the bottom of each ear as this will be felted into the neck to give a nice secure attachment. The ears can be alert or more relaxed: I have given these a rather relaxed stance, so sticking out slightly and leaning backwards a little. Alert ears would be more upright and leaning forward more.

When happy with their location, begin felting around the back of the ears in a semi-circle to attach them to the head. Felt well into the head so that the attachment is sound, then remove the pins. The ears are now attached but will need some tweaking; particularly a little more shaping to both sides of the bottom edge, so take a little more Antique Merino tops and felt on a tiny triangle that runs from the inside bottom edge of the ear, onto the top of the head and slightly around to the other side of the ear, as shown in image 21. This is a fairly easy process if you gently felt onto the ear first, then onto the head, and then build in-between, using your finger to guide you around the inside. Image 22 shows the difference of one completed and one not. Do the same to the outside bottom edges, felting a smaller triangle inward.

23

Step 8
23-25

Felt a line for the mouth and make a shallow cut at an angle so that the top lip slopes down over the bottom. Don't cut level, but at a 45 degree angle downward. Felt on a black nose with Raven Merino tops, and place two small, round-headed pins for the nostrils. Tightly felt around them with the Raven tops and cut two little slits, one each side of the nostrils, about a third of the way from the bottom of the nose (not halfway). Felt in-between the cuts to refine these. Add more wool as needed to obtain a good nose shaping. Trim the surface to make it as fuzz-free and smooth as possible. (Refer to nose creation in the Chihuahua chapter, page 30.)

24

Step 9
26

Cover half of the underbelly area with a fine layer of Candy Floss, leaving a small area of pink between the front legs. As this won't necessarily show through the fur, unless making a Yorkie with a fine coat this step can be missed.

25

Step 10
27, 28

The coat comes next. Yorkies can have a range of colours and patterns, from black to pale grey and rich rust to pale fawn. Some have grey down their legs; others just have a grey saddle. Once decided, use one of the alcohol pens to mark the coat pattern, ensuring it is equal on both sides (these lines will not show once the fur is

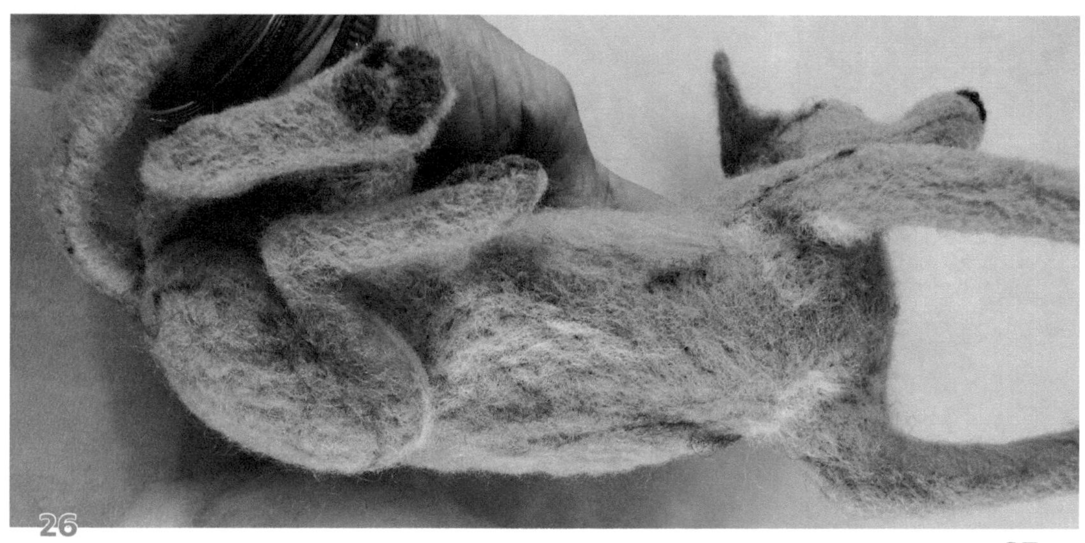

26

27

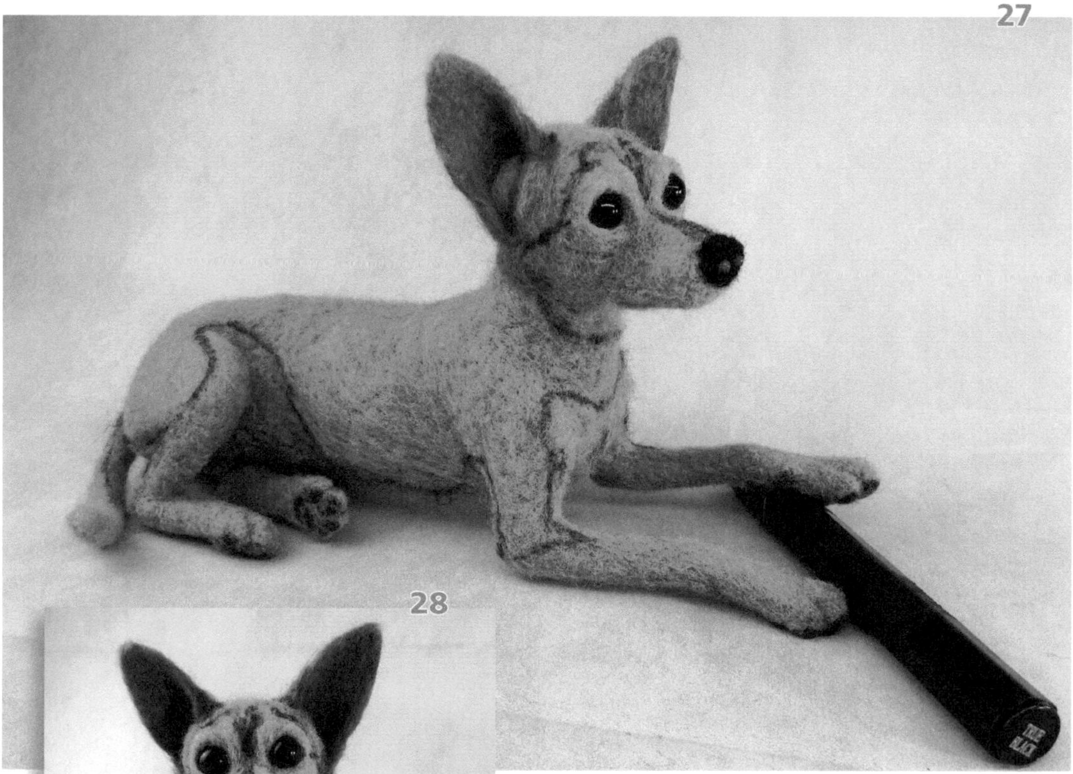

28

attached). The demarcation line between colours is a guide only, and, as you will see, the colours change gradually rather than abruptly, so more blending will be needed between them.

Step 11
29, 30

For this dog's coat I am using four colours

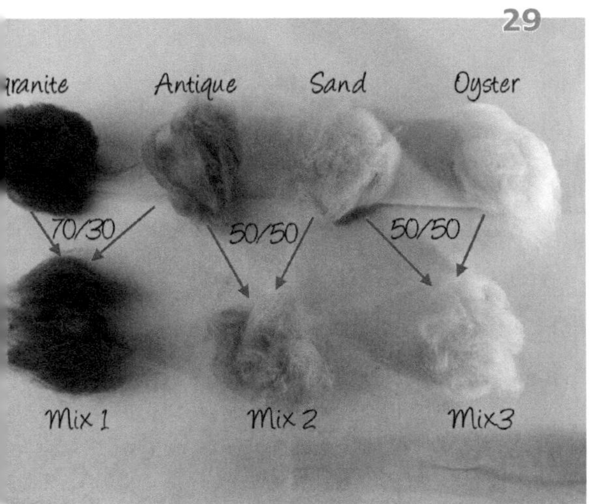

of Merino: Oyster, Sand, Antique, and Granite .

Begin by cutting the tops into lengths of between 6cm (2.36in) and 7cm (2.75in). Card each colour to separate the fibres and make them workable. To create the subtle tones required for this particular coat colouring, blend the following –
70:30 Granite with Antique (Mix 1)
50:50 Antique with Sand (Mix 2)
50:50 Sand with Oyster (Mix 3)

– and you will have two shades of grey and five shades of dark to light brown: seven shades out of four original colours. Of course, you can mix various proportions to obtain even more hue: I haven't used the black for mixing but would if creating a darker-coated Yorkie.

TIP
If using small, metal-toothed carders, blend only half thicknesses of tops at a time: take the cut lengths (before carding) and divide in half; card, then add the other colour, also divided in half, and blend. If you try and blend too much in one go, it won't work. Better to use small amounts and blend well

A detailed description of how to blend can be found in the Blending chapter of the book

Step 12
31

To get a rough idea of where each colour will be placed, refer to the colour map image 31, overleaf, where colours meet, lightly blend both along the line so that the colour change is gradual. Now you should have enough of the wool blends ready to make a good start, your dog marked out, and a colour map to refer to so are ready to attach the fur.

Step 12
32, 33

Before starting, double-check that you have enough blended colours to work from and won't run out: have a little of a blended colour spare so that you have something to match up with.

Important: Don't attempt complex long fur blending and attachment in poor lighting, as you will inevitably make mistakes that will become glaringly apparent in daylight! I have had to pull out many a coat and start again because of doing this.

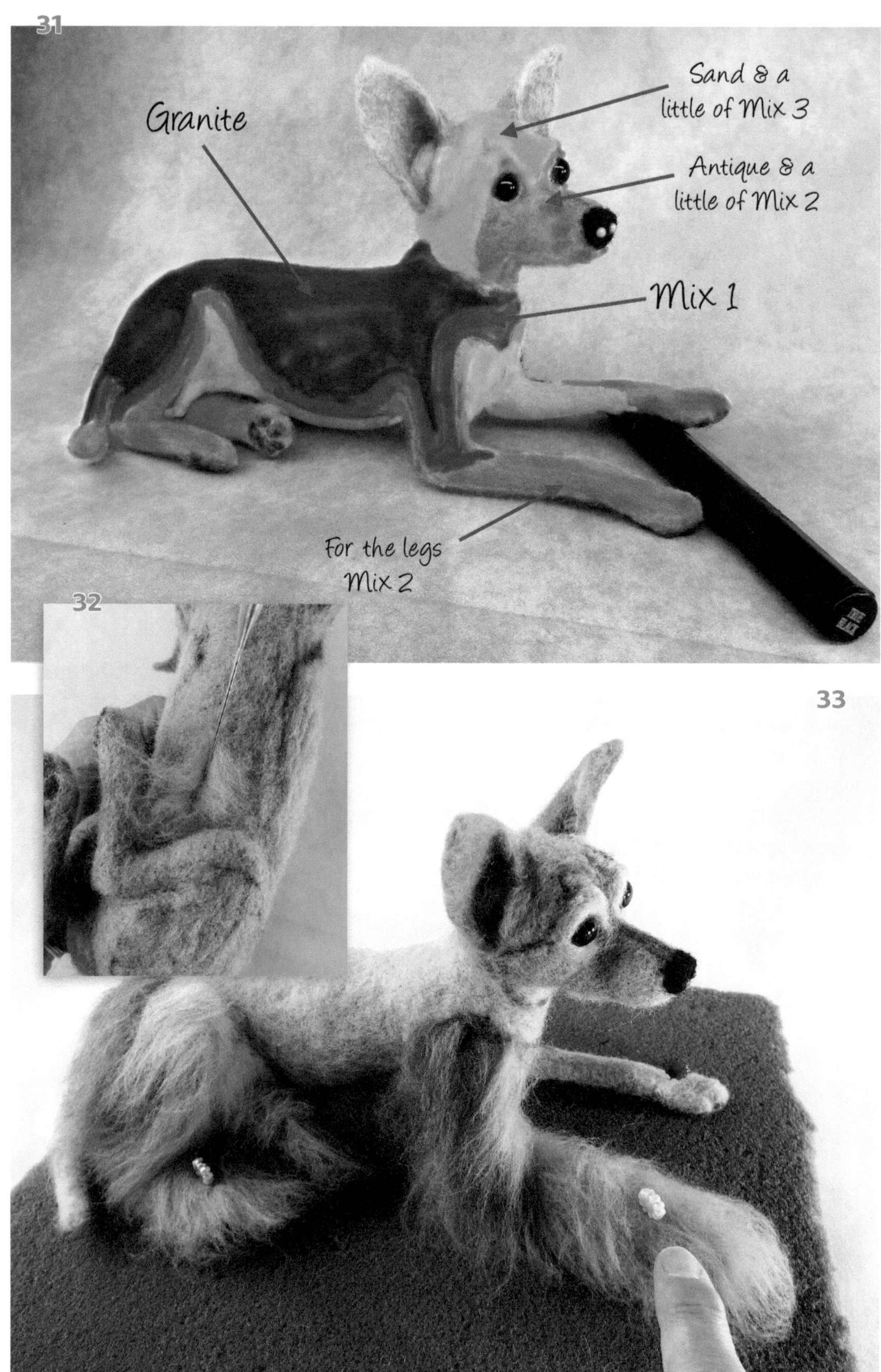
31
Granite
Sand & a
little of Mix 3
Antique & a
little of Mix 2
Mix 1
For the legs
Mix 2
32
33

Starting, as always at the bottom and working up, attach Mix 3 to the belly area and between the back legs, using the 'down the centre' attachment method for this part. Don't try and felt on too much at once, but rather fine (almost see-through) amounts. Now, working from the bottom to the top, start by attaching long fur to the paws, using Mix 2 and felting on the end of each attachment method, making sure you attach smaller amounts of wool to each toe. In fact, a small, awl-thickness amount of wool would suffice and make for easier work. You won't be able to attach thick lengths of wool – it just won't be possible – so as long as your attachments are fairly easy to do, you know you have the right thickness.

Cover the toes and paws and work your way up the legs, paying attention to the colour change to Sand and some Mix 3 on the insides of the legs. Completely cover the leg, laying the attachments in the direction of hair growth; try not to disturb what you have already done as you work. Which method of wool attachment used on the body is up to you – down the centre or on the end of each length, whichever you find the easiest and gives the best results. Remember to pay attention to the direction of hair growth, and note that the legs will look nothing like they do on the finished sculpture, until trimmed.

34

Step 13
34, 35

With the underbelly and legs covered, pin the sculpture onto a felting sponge/mat to help stabilise it whilst you work on the body and head.

With coat marking lines, take a small amount of the two colours concerned and make another blend with these: this will enable the colour change to be much softer. The Yorkie coat doesn't usually show a well-defined line between two colours but a graduated one, especially once the animal is an adult. Create this blend along and between all lines of colour change. Continue over the back with Granite.

If you wish you can gently clip the fur lengths, but not too harshly: only to make

35

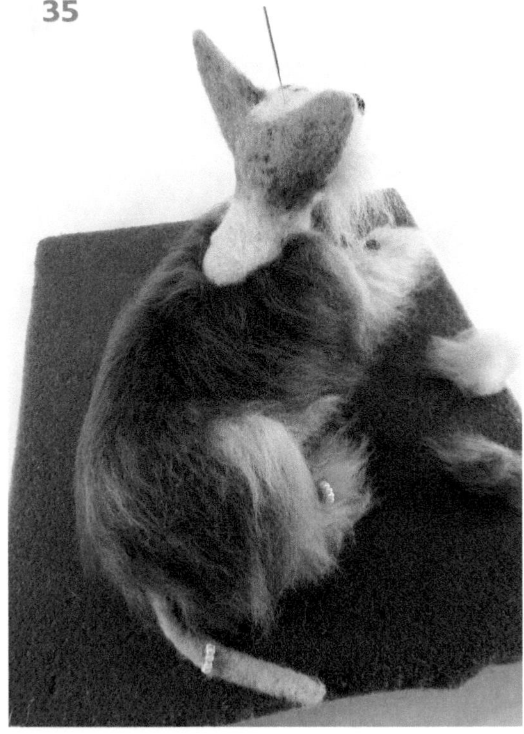

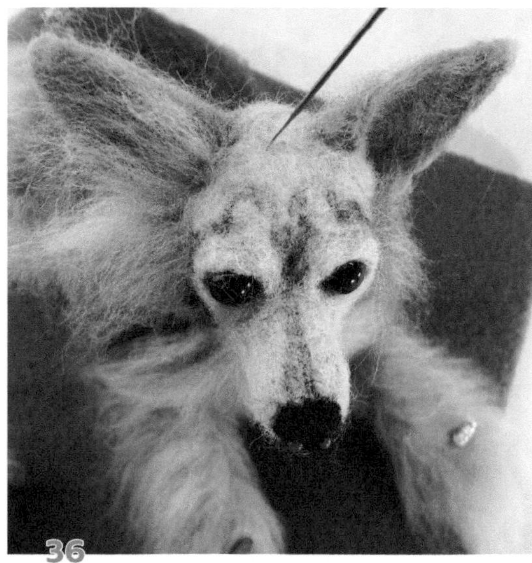
36

37

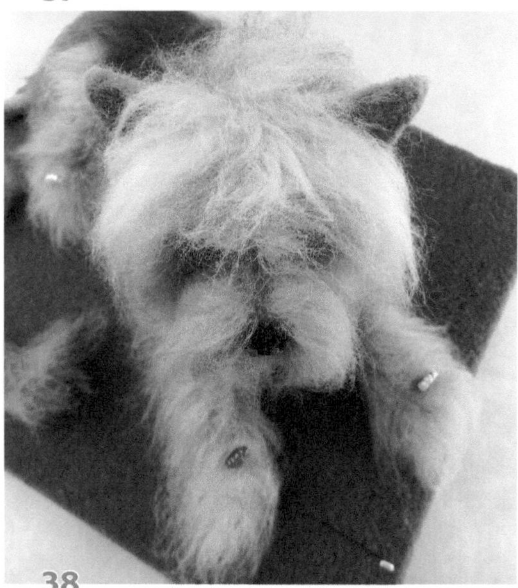
38

it more manageable. Don't forget to gently tease the fur in the direction of natural growth. Leave the neck free from fur at this stage to make it possible to work on the head and head detail without flattening the neck fur each time. This area can easily wait until last, as can the tail.

Step 14
36-38

Begin adding long fur at the back of the head and work forwards. Head fur tends to lay backwards and downwards, so starting at the front would mean having to constantly lift fur just attached, rather than attach over what's been added, and it doesn't make for nice and even attachment.

Head markings will have been made with an alcohol pen, so will denote where the tan and grey go. **Note:** Whilst I made markings on this sculpture for grey fur on the head, I actually decided not to add any; instead, making the head all-tan. Remember to soften the lines between the colours and graduate them by mixing the two colours used. Note that around the top frame of the head, in front of the ears, the fur is slightly lighter: use some of Mix 3 here. and don't forget to graduate it as it becomes darker around the eyes and down the muzzle. Pay careful attention when attaching fur around the eyes and nose. and felt in the attachments gently. Felt in long fur right up around the eyes, ensuring it lays in the correct position/ direction.

Step 15
39

Having attached fur around the eyes, pop out the spacer beads and gently colour the inside of the eyelid black. When the ink is dry, refit the spacer beads and make

39

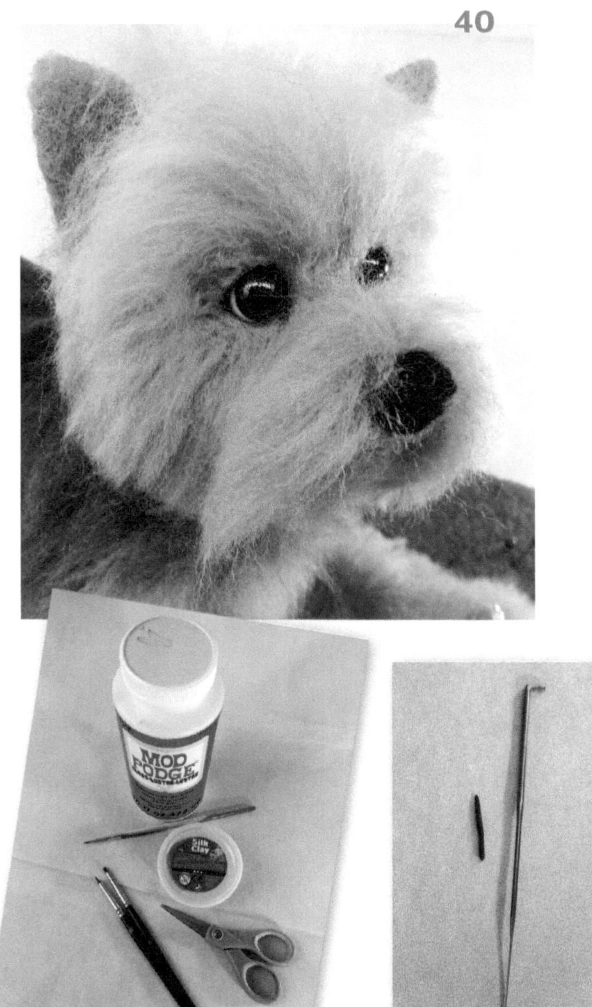

40

41

42

a final check for eyelid size and shape: a perfect fit and shape is shown in image 40. Adjust if needed and add more long fur around the eye if required. A little clipping of the head fur will be needed at this stage before you can add the Silk Clay eyelids. Fit the final eyes and glue in place. Allow to dry.

Fit the eyes that you coloured in Step 5 and glue in place.

Step 16
40-44

Using Mod Podge Gloss, a fine paintbrush, scissors, and small clay modelling tools, make the eyelids as described in previous chapters. Paint the inner eyelid with Mod Podge Gloss, roll out a fine length of SilK Clay – around 1mm (0.039in) thick and 1.5cm (0.59in) long – and apply the first length to either the upper or lower eyelid area. Mould into place with the clay modelling tools; then repeat for the other eyelids. Allow to dry.

43

Step 17
45, 46

With the eyelids dry, build up the fur

44

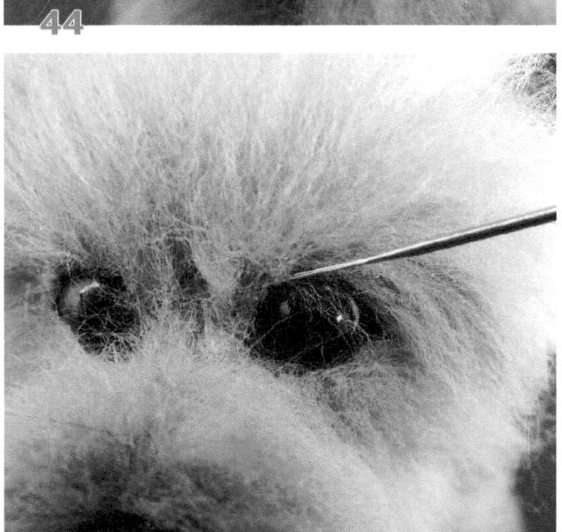
45

46

around them to make a seamless joint. Do this VERY carefully with a fine needle, adding only fine amounts of fibre at a time. Do not poke the needle into the eyelids, but alongside them. One eye surround completed on the right side, the other to be done is shown in image 46.

Also at this stage give the nose a coating of Mod Podge, ensuring there are a couple of small, round-headed pins in the nostrils to keep them open. Avoid getting Mod Podge on the pins. Leave to dry.

Step 18
47

Complete the long fur attachment on the tail now – paying attention to the colour

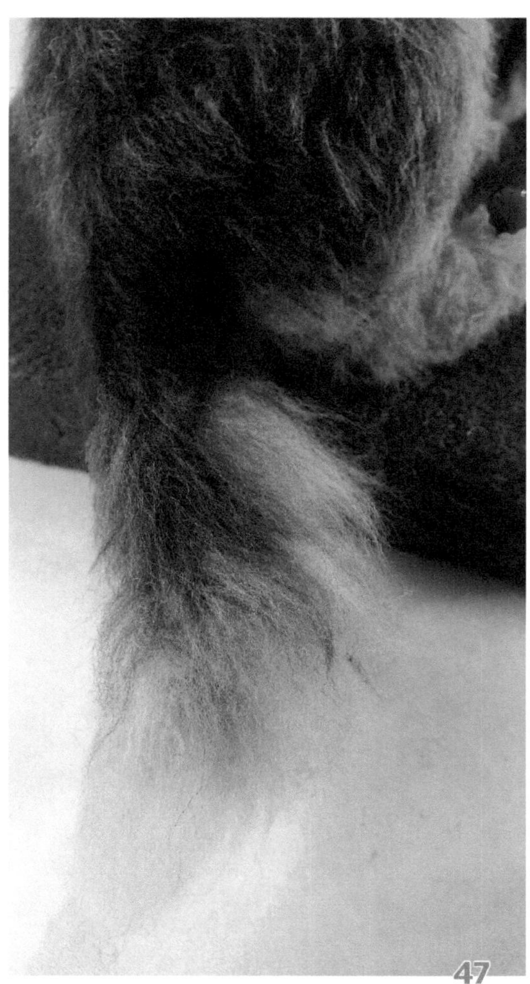
47

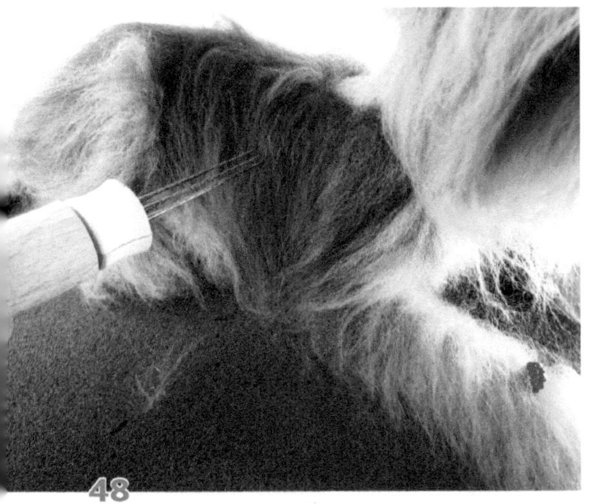

48

49

50

51

pattern and changes – or leave this until Step 21, where it is explained in a little more detail.

Step 19
48-52

With all of the long fur attached (except around the neck: check there is enough blended wool to complete this later), the first clipping is next on the agenda. To prepare for this you will need a quad multi-needle or, as I am using in the photo, a 3-needle tool.

Gently tease the fur in the direction of hair growth. As you do this, stray fibres will come loose, which is completely normal; clumps, however, should never come loose. If they do, you haven't felted them in far enough. For the gentle combing, I favour a 3-needle tool, with the needles in a straight line, and is very effective for this job.

52

Clipping can be done several ways – short all over but fluffy around the face; long around the legs, but short on the body – but whichever you decide on, clip only small amounts first. With the fur combed into place, take small, sharp pointed scissors and begin trimming the edges in the direction of fur growth (mostly downward). This will give a nice natural finish. Don't be tempted at this stage to make a deep clip, because if too much is removed it will be necessary to pull out the cut fur and felt in replacement wool. I never seem to manage fewer than five clips on my dogs, and often do more. Note that Yorkie hair isn't all one length, especially if a coat has been maintained by a dog groomer, so there will be different lengths on the legs, body and face.

As you clip, re-comb and arrange with the 3-needle tool (see above). This is a very messy procedure and cleaning up with a velvet clothes brush will keep the work area tidy. Don't forget to un-pin your sculpture from the felting sponge/mat and clip underneath. This should be easy to do when you hold the sculpture by the clear neck area. Once done, pin down again to stabilise the sculpture as you continue to chip.

Pay attention to the different lengths of fur on the face, which is often very short under the eyes, long on top of the head, trimmed neatly around the top of the eyes and long each side of the muzzle, but shorter around the front of the mouth and along the top of the muzzle.

Step 20
53-56

Now for the really fun part, texturing the coat! How to tame and texture a long coat made entirely of unruly Merino wool remains a mystery to many, but my secret weapon is L'Oreal Elnett Satin aerosol-free, pump-action hairspray.

Once happy with your final clip, spray sections of the coat with a light dusting of hairspray. Using the 3-needle tool, begin to texturize the coat into waves and quiffs, paying attention to direction of hair growth. The fur will look wet at first, but once textured with the 3-needle tool, the fibres will separate and look more natural once dry. Continue in sections. Shield the eyes before spraying as they must be kept clean for their final coat of Diamond Glaze. You might also need to do the odd bit of trimming as you texture the coat.

TIP

Spraying too gently will result in blobs of hairspray on the fibre but, if this happens, gently soak up the excess with kitchen paper. Aim to spray firmly and evenly to achieve a fine coverage: practice on paper first to see how the spray behaves. You can also spray and texture the coat more than once

53

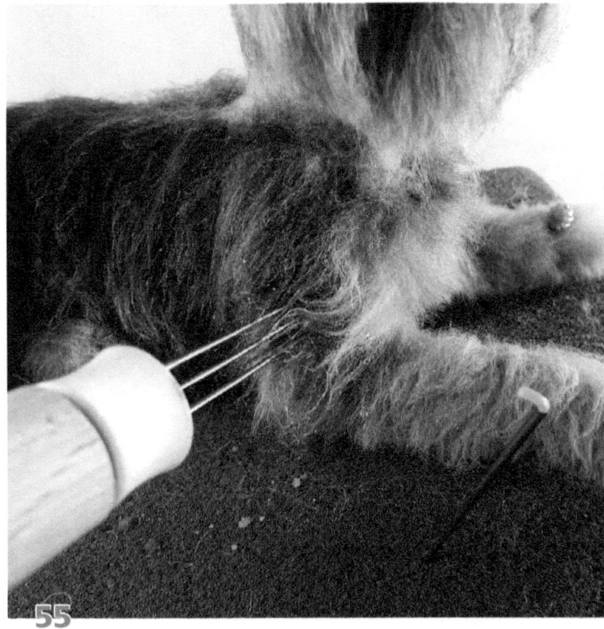
55

54

56

Finishing touches might include colouring areas of fur, especially around the face and mouth, using Spectrum Noir pens – EB3 first followed by the slightly darker EB8. Add colouring around the mouth, nose and eyes; gradually at first to assess where extra colouring is needed, and what you want to achieve. Bold marking will look ugly and obvious, so less is best

Step 21
57

With the coat textured and head completed, add fur around the neck and tail (if you haven't already done the tail). Make the top of the tail the same colouring as the body, and the underneath the same as the legs. Before you start covering the tail, you might need to add a little more core wool around it to which long fur can be easily attached.

57

58

Use the end of length attachment method rather than the down the centre method, as this will give the tail a longer length of fur. Carefully blend the colours where they meet. Trim and texture.

59

Step 22
58, 59

To complete the nose, file its surface to smooth the hardened Mod Podge, and finalise nose shape and detail by cutting a couple of slits each side. Gently file into shape. Add another layer of sealant to make a smoother finish. Allow to dry, file the surface and add another layer of sealant, then file again if needed. Lastly, apply a good covering of Spectrum Noir Black.

Step 23
60-64

With the texturing done and fur clipped into shape, apply the final covering of eye gloss. Completely clear the eye surface of any stray fibres (even one stray fibre will spoil the gloss coating). Use a large soft paintbrush to brush the surrounding fur away from the eye, and brush away any loose fibres, then clip away any that keep springing back onto the eye. With the eyes completely clear, dampen the fine, soft paintbrush and apply Diamond Glaze to

60

61

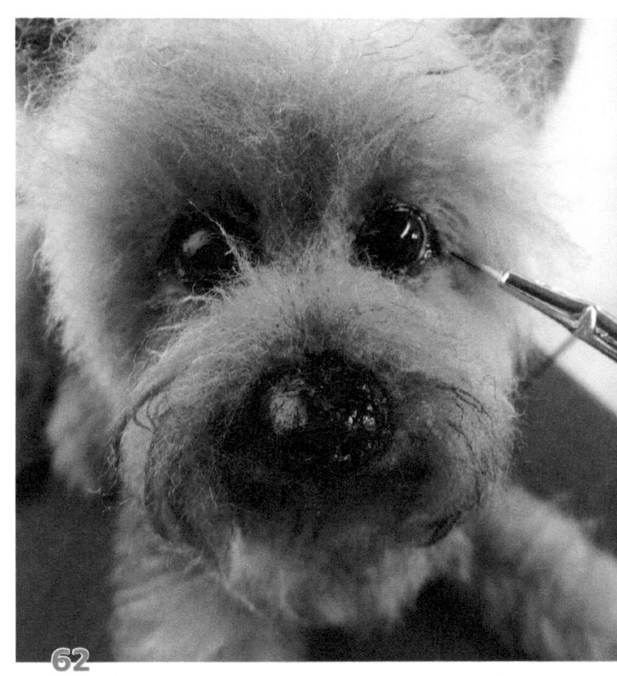

62

each eye in clean strokes. It might help to put a dab of glaze onto a piece of tin foil to make it easier to apply. Don't be tempted to keep going over the yes with the brush as the glaze starts to dry quite quickly. Be sure to cover the eyelids, too, on the inside

63

64

edge and both corners of each eye to give the appearance of fluid in the eye. Allow to dry before doing anything else.

An extra touch is to spray hairspray onto foil and apply around the mouth with a thin brush, which gives the appearance of wet fur around the mouth.

Once dry, rearrange the face fur naturally and you're done!

Making the bowl of dog food is covered in the Accessories chapter.

THE POODLE

In this chapter you will learn how to create a curly-coated dog. The chapter will highlight the curly coat, clipping, colouring, texturing, larger eyes and a wax nose. I have covered two types of clip in this chapter: a Teddy Clip for the off-white Poodle, and a Miami Clip for the black Poodle.

A wide range of 2-, 3- and 4-ply knitting wool/acyclic mix exists that would work for this sculpture. The important requirement is that the wool has a good 'crimp' that isn't lost when the ply is separated.

YOU WILL NEED

Materials (black Poodle)

- Wire, 16-gauge 1 x 37cm (14.5in) & 2 x 34cm (13.38in)
- Core (black), 80g (2.82oz)
- Any chunky black knitting wool with a good 'crimp'
- Small amount of mid-grey Merino
- 2 x 8mm (0.31in) spacer beads, preferably light so they are easily seen
- 2 x off-white acrylic 8mm (0.31in) beads for the eyes
- Silk Clay, black

- Diamond Glaze
- Two small, round-headed pins
- Mod Podge, Satin & Gloss
- Alcohol pens: EB8, IG10, TN7

Materials (white Poodle)

- Wire, 16-gauge 1 x 37cm (14.5in) and 2 x 34cm (13.38in)
- Core (white), 80g (2.82oz)
- Any chunky white or off-white knitting wool with a good 'crimp'
- 2 x 10mm (0.39in) spacer beads, preferably dark so they are easily seen
- 2 x black acrylic 10mm (0.39in) beads for the eyes
- Silk Clay, black
- Diamond Glaze
- Two small, round-headed pins
- Mod Podge, Satin & Gloss
- Alcohol pens: Black, BG6, EB5, EB8, TN7, IG10, GB9

Tools

- Wire cutters
- Awl
- Pliers
- Tape measure/ruler
- Nail file
- Range of single felting needles
- A 3-needle tool
- 4in pointed scissors, and larger ones for cutting the 4-ply wool

- 6mm (0.23in) circle template 6mm
- Fine (nail art-type) paintbrush
- Kitchen roll; small glass of water
- Clay modelling tools, small, rubber-tipped
- Felting brush
- Multi-needle (sprung-type)

2

Step 1
1

I started out making a black Poodle, but getting good photos was problematic, so I also made an off-white example to show alongside it. The methods for both colours of Poodle are exactly the same: they differ only in minor details and the final clip; these differences are mentioned in the relevant steps.

Decide which of the colours you'd like your Poodle to be, and gather together what you need by way of materials. Use the wire lengths to create the armature as shown in image 1, and bend to given measurements. Pose and stand square the armature, and trim excess from paws to make them 0.5cm (0.19in) long.

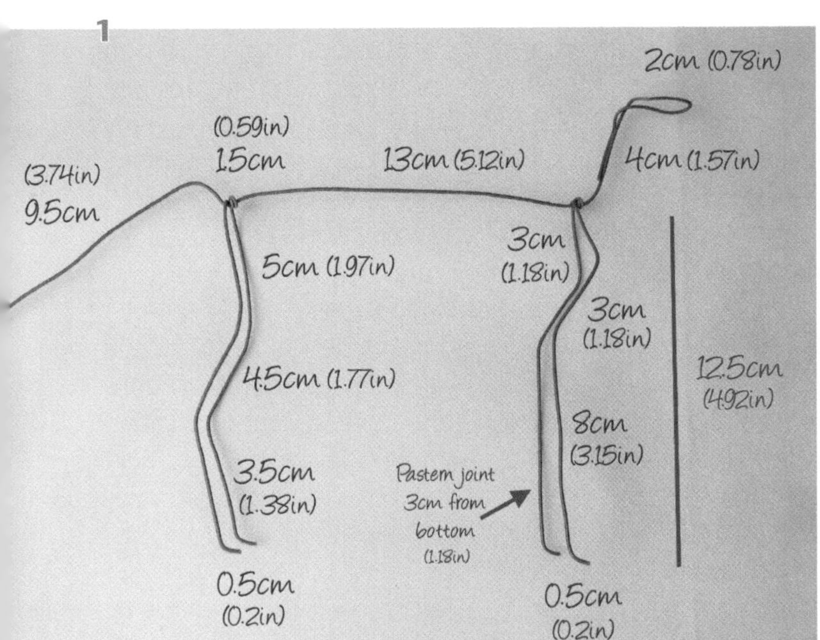

Step 2
2, 3

Make a first covering of either black or white core wool; then add bulk, shape and definition of your choice. This sculpture is based on the Toy Poodle, which often tends to have a slightly arched back. Work on the face detail and make indents where the eyes will go. Add grey Merino wool pads to the paws for the white Poodle: no need to add any for the black Poodle, as they won't be very visible.

Felt the paws firmly to take the extra wool that will be attached later.

TIP
Google images of clipped Poodles to get an idea of body shape

Step 3
4, 5

With this sculpture I've added the head whilst creating the body and

3

4

not made it separately. As a rough guide, overall head length should be around 5.5cm (2.16in) from back of head to tip of completed nose.

Once you have a good head and face shape, it's time to fit the 10mm (0.39in) spacer beads, using the same method as in previous chapters. Make a horizontal slit that is in-line with the top of the muzzle, and roughly 7mm (0.27in) deep and 8mm (0.31in) wide. Open up with the scissors and coax the spacer bead into place. It should be a tight fit and not pop out when touched. Only one-third of the eye should be exposed, with the other two-thirds covered. Once the spacer beads are secure, begin building up around the eyes so that they are equal shapes and thicknesses. To help with this, look at your work both right way up and upside down.

*Create a black core wool felt nose on the muzzle, and place two small, round-headed pins for the nostrils, working a shape around them. Felt the nose as hard as you can, and don't be afraid to use the scissors to trim into shape. Cut two slits each side of the nostrils and felt in the edges to tidy them. Give a final trim.

*For both colour dogs you can create a Silk Clay nose, as follows. Mould a very basic felt nose, without any features, of the correct size and overall shape, to ensure correct muzzle length and nose location. Carefully cut off this nose, cutting evenly on both sides, taking care not to cut away any more than where the nose would be. If you do cut away too much, build back up with white core.

The reason for cutting off the felted nose is to create a perfect cavity for the Silk Clay nose, which isn't as easily done by making the nose straight on to the end of the muzzle. This method allows the correct amount of surrounding muzzle for the nose, to help it sit correctly and be in proportion.

Add a small dab of PVA glue to the nose cavity, ensuring it doesn't spill over. Take a small piece of black Silk Clay, enough to create a nose, and squish it into the nose cavity to ensure it is embedded into the glue, cavity and wool, adding more clay to fashion the nose if needed. You will have to work quickly to make a nose as the small amounts of clay used will dry quickly: dabbing the clay with a damp brush will delay this a little, but don't make it too wet, as it will then be sticky to work with.

Use the modelling tools to create the nose, following the basic pattern in image 5, after which you can define the details. Work with the nose upside-down as well as right way up, as this will help to keep it equal in shape and size. Create the final texture of the nose with a fine pointed tool, making small, close together indents, or lightly press the surface with an emery board/nail file to add texture. If you're not happy with the nose for any reason, simply pull it out and start again!

When the nose is dry, fill any gaps between the Silk Clay and the wool and felt in; then trim. With glue add a fine line of white core wool around the edges of the nose, to give the appearance of fur growing on the surrounding skin. Allow to dry and trim, creating a seamless join between muzzle and nose.

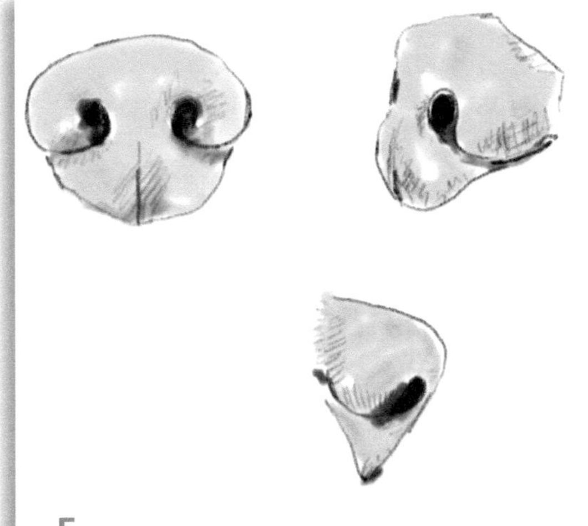

5

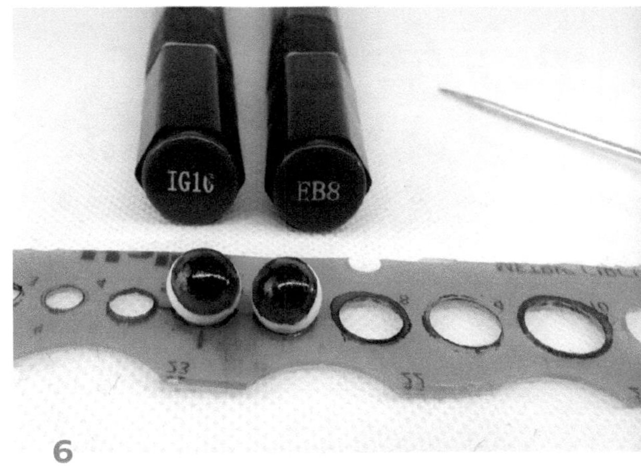

6

Make a shallow cut for the mouth and, if making an off-white Poodle, felt a small amount of black wool inside it.

Step 4

6

Using an 8mm (0.31in) circle template colour the off-white beads, firstly with the EB8 pen, completely covering inside the circle in a circular motion, starting on the outside edge and working inward. Once covered, leave to dry. Use IG10 for the pupils, dotting the colour on and not allowing it over the brown as this will wipe away what you have already done. Allow to dry and give a covering of Diamond Glaze.

Allow to dry and add more colour detail as needed, making the pupil blur into the iris colouring using additional TN7 colouring. With this pen add another light colouring around the very edge of the iris to define it, or very carefully with EB8. Allow ink to dry and cover with Diamond Glaze. Allow to dry. You may need to touch up some details. Give another coating of Diamond Glaze to protect the beads. Allow to dry completely.

Step 5

7

When the eye sockets are the correct shape, fit the final eyes; first adding a line

7

of colouring with the black pen to the inside of each eye socket for the white Poodle. **Important:** Allow the ink to dry BEFORE fitting the eyes.

With the ink in the eye socket dry, insert each eye without glue to check for fit, that they look the same, and the eye openings are the correct shape and size, remembering that they need to be slightly more open at this stage to accommodate the Silk Clay eyelids still to come. Ideally, the top and bottom of the openings should just overlap the top and bottom of the iris on the bead. Set aside the eyes until later and refit the spacer beads.

The black Poodle won't require face colour with alcohol pens as this would not show against the black wool.

8

Step 6

8

For the black Poodle I used Robin Super Chunky 2-ply, and for the off-white Poodle I used 4-ply Cable Knit M000671 from B&M Stores. The larger balls of wool will easily cover three or more dogs of this size.

Step 7

9, 10

Start by deciding what sort of clip you want, as this will dictate the length of wool for different areas. Google the different clips as there are many to choose from, both Asian and Western. Image 9: For the off-white Poodle I have chosen an Asian style, with a teddy bear face clip.

Image 10: For the black Poodle I have chosen a Miami clip with long trousers for the bottom half of the legs, and with a slightly shorter body clip and a clean muzzle, with a top knot and fluffy ears (you don't have to have a bowed top knot, of course). Because the length of fur varies over both dogs, cut the wool accordingly. For these sculptures we are using the

9

10

attach down the centre of each length method, rather than the attach at the end of each length method, because this fibre is slightly stronger than the Merino and will attach more easily using the centre method than the end method.

Once you have determined the end length of coat in any particular area, the lengths of wool required will be double that measurement plus 1cm (0.39in) to allow for attachment and clipping. So a finished coat length of 2cm (0.78in) would require 2 + 2 + 1 = 5cm (1.9in) of wool for attachment. Alternatively, you could keep it simple and attach the same length all over and clip, but that method means a lot of wastage.

Step 8
11

Prepare the fibre lengths by splitting the ply. For the off-white Poodle I'm using a 4-ply, so this will need to be split into 4, and then each ply will need to be split in half, resulting in eight lengths of fibre from one cut length of 4-ply wool. Do the splitting gently so that the fibres hold together nicely and retain their 'crimp,' which will give the lovely Poodle coat.

With a 2-ply wool, split in half to make two, then again to give four lengths. For finer areas such as paws and around the face and eyes, etc, lengths must be split in half again to make them fine enough to attach. The cutting and splitting of wool is a very therapeutic exercise, and you might like to prepare a decent number so that you don't have to keep stopping to make more. I prepare and store some in a plastic container with a lid.

TIP

When cutting the wool, don't do so if it's under tension, otherwise some

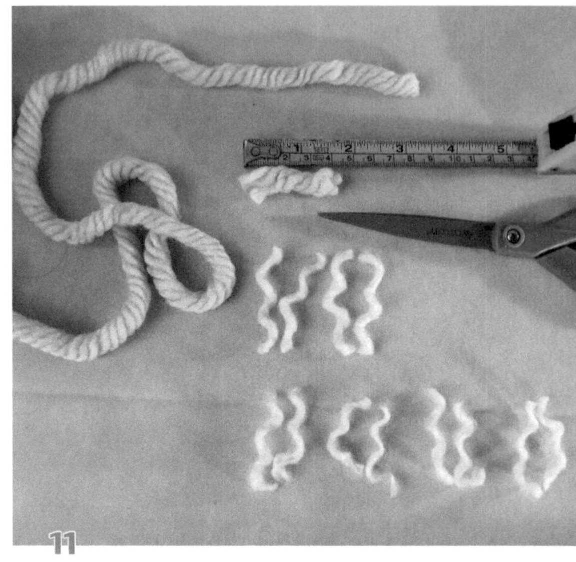

11

lengths will be much shorter than they should be

Step 9
12-14

To attach the wool, begin at the bottom and work upward, starting with the shortest and finest lengths of wool for the paws, as these will be cut short when you clip. Take a length and lay it across where you want it to go (shown in the images with black on white, and on the body so that it's clearly visible), and felt it down

12

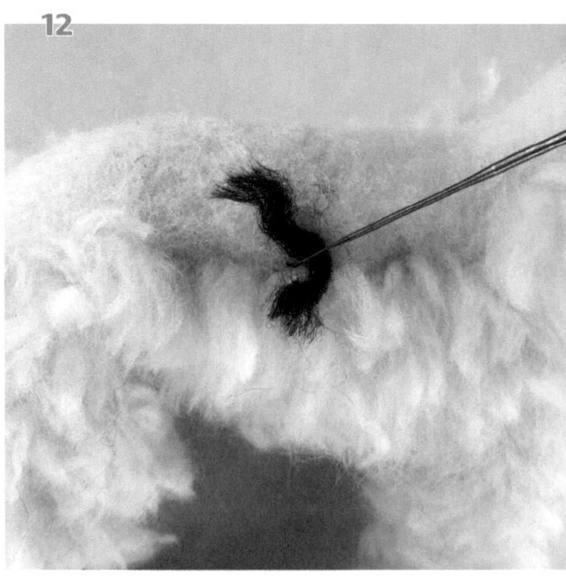

13

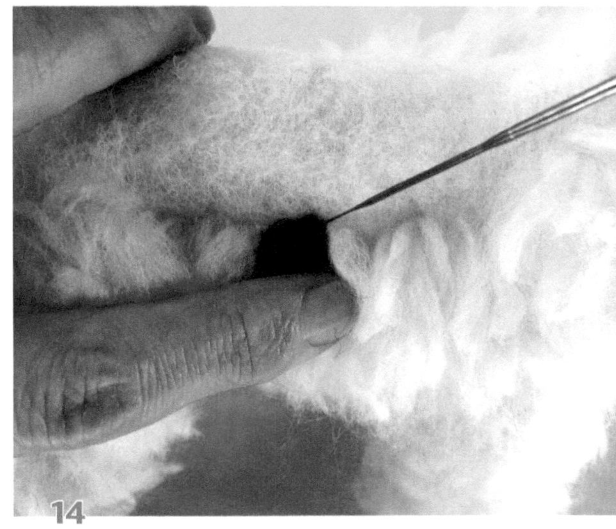

14

the centre so that it rises up each side and comes together as it is felted into the sculpture's surface.

When you have a good attachment, fold down one side and lightly felt both ends into position along the surface of the sculpture. You only need to do this lightly; just enough to keep the fibres in place so that they don't spring back in the way of the next attachment.

Step 10
15-18

Once the paws have been covered with the shorter fibre lengths, begin adding longer lengths up the legs, in keeping with the

15

16

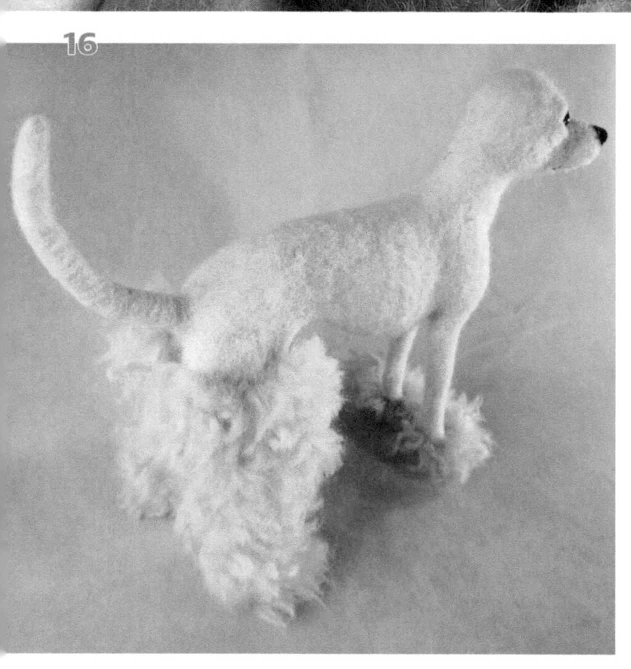

17

18

chosen coat length. Continue to cover the body, up the legs, over the belly and body, paying attention to coat length. The white Poodle coat is the same length overall, but the black Poodle has longer lengths on the legs. Be sure to make the attachments close together so there are no gaps. When you reach the neck, leave it clear until the end so that there is somewhere to hold when handling the sculpture without damaging the rest of the coat.

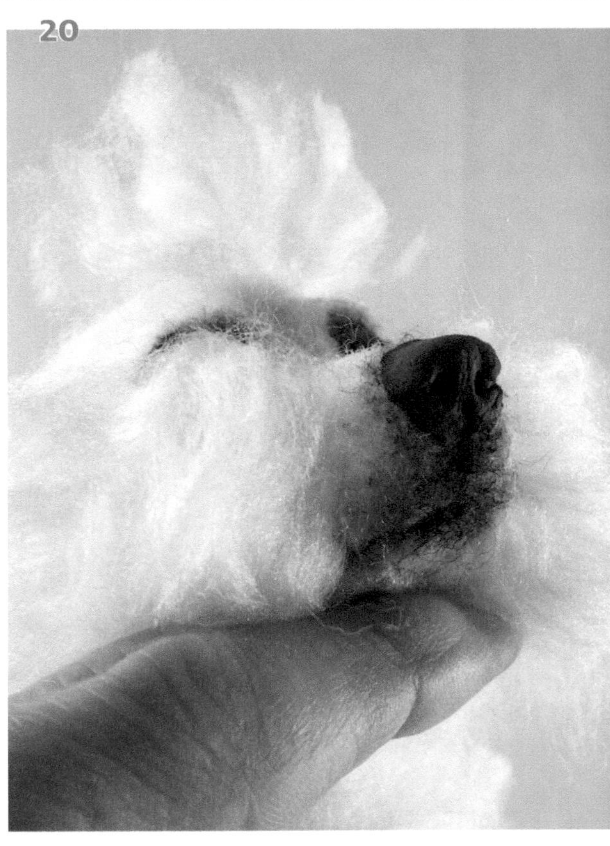
20

Step 11
19, 20

With most of the body covered, start on the head. Work from the bottom of the head upward, making sure to leave two areas to attach the ears. For the white Poodle, before adding wool to the muzzle, lightly colour around the bottom and on the top of the nose with Spectrum Noir pen IG10. As you add finer attachments of wool over this area, you will notice that this colouring gives a more realistic look of darker skin under the fur. You can also tweak the finer coverage of wool in this area by reverse felting around the nose over the coloured areas. Around the muzzle, for the off-white teddy clip, use 4cm (1.57in) lengths, but split further as you did for the paws and top of the head into 5cm (1.96in) lengths.

19

For the black Poodle use 2cm (0.78in) lengths around the muzzle and bottom half of the face, and 4cm (1.57in) lengths for the top of the head. Around the muzzle much finer lengths of wool should be used, especially around the eyes and nose attach with a fine needle. Add wool right up to the edge of the nose and a little way around the eyes. Eyelids will be required before completing adding wool around the eyes. Leave two spaces for ear attachment. The very short wool attachments for this Miami clip on the face cover the muzzle and all of the head except the top. Anything above the eyes on top of the head (the top knot) is longer wool.

Step 12
21

The ears are the same shape for both Poodles. On a felting brush and with a sprung multi-needle tool, felt two ear shapes, roughly 5cm (1.96in) long and 4cm (1.57in) wide at the widest point. Leave a free edge along the top as this will be used to attach to the head. Felt a decent thickness, but not so thick that it won't fold easily. Lift off the brush with an awl and alternately felt down both sides until well felted. Tidy around the bottom edge with a single needle.

When the ears are complete, prepare and split 5cm (1.96in) lengths of wool as you did earlier, and begin attaching these around the bottom edge of the ear. Lay each length across where it should go, and felt down the centre, then fold flat the attachment and felt along the top of the bend to ensure the wool lays flat, and is hanging in the right direction. Now turn over the ear and felt another layer around the bottom edge in the same way (this will cover the ear shape under the fur). Once you have covered the edge, turn over again and continue to cover the rest of the ear almost up to the top, with 7cm (2.75in) of prepared wool in the same way to cover the ears (remember to leave clear the top 1cm (0.39in) as this will be used to attach the ear to the head, and any additional fur attachment will be done with the ear attached.

You should then have two ears, the insides with a line of fur attachment around the inner edge, and the outsides almost all covered with long fur.

For the black Poodle, the lengths of wool are longer on the ears – 10cm (3.93in) – so once attached will hang roughly 5cm long (1.96in) once clipped.

Step 13
22-25

To attach the ears, hold one upright with the full fur attachment facing inward onto the back of the head. Place the top part of the ear (the fuzzy, un-felted part) onto the side of the head, and fold forward the back bottom corner onto the rest of the ear, as shown. Pin in position, and do the same with the other ear, ensuring both are equally positioned, in the same direction and of the same length.

Assess length and position by folding forward the ears onto the head to see how they look. Felt securely in place, then fold down and felt into place around the top of the ear, so that it holds its position when you release it. Now add the remaining fur to the bald

21

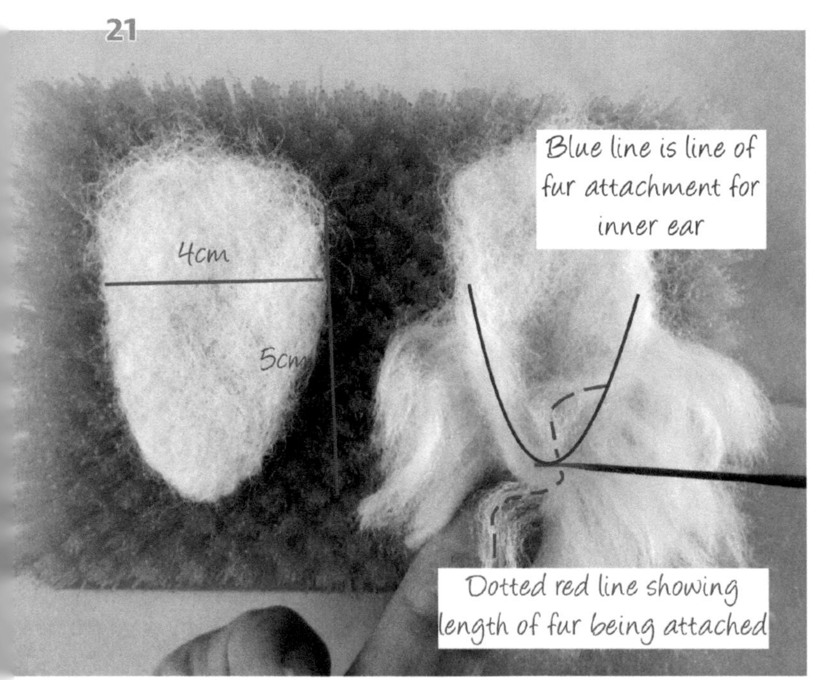

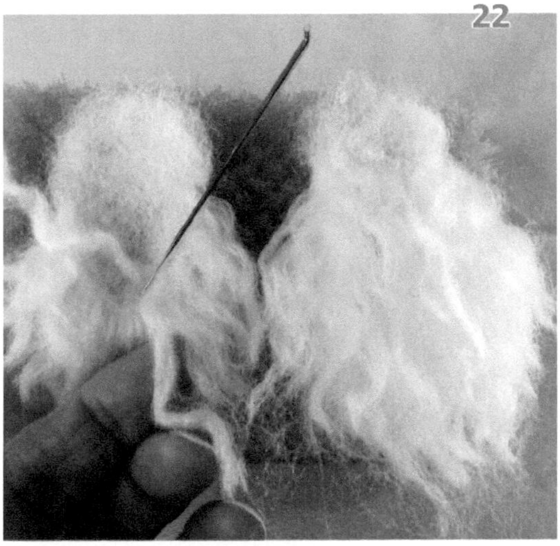

22

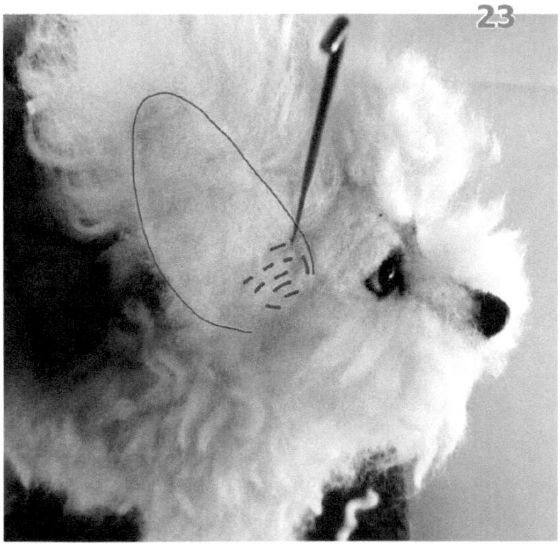

23

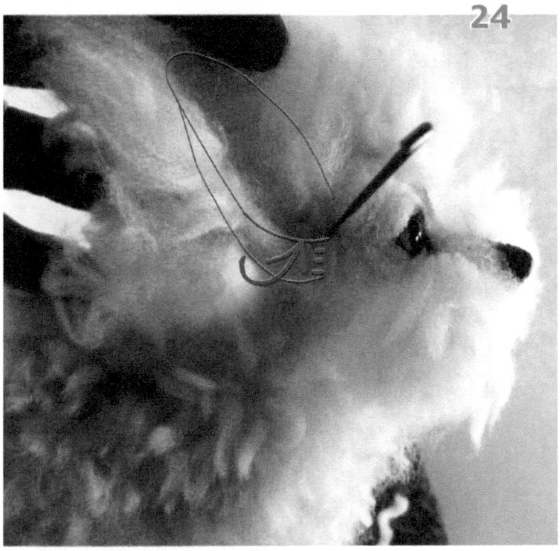

24

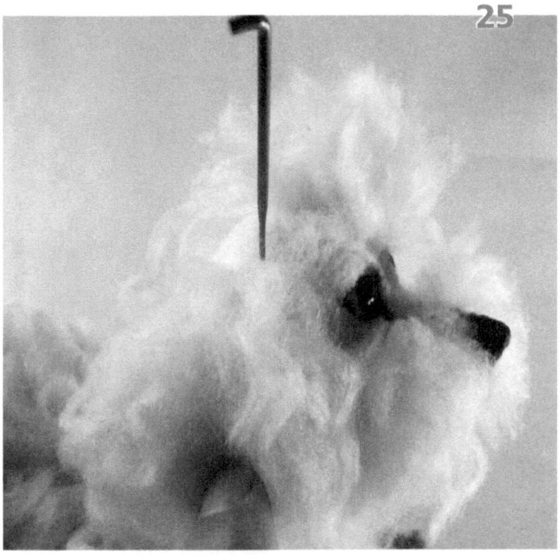

25

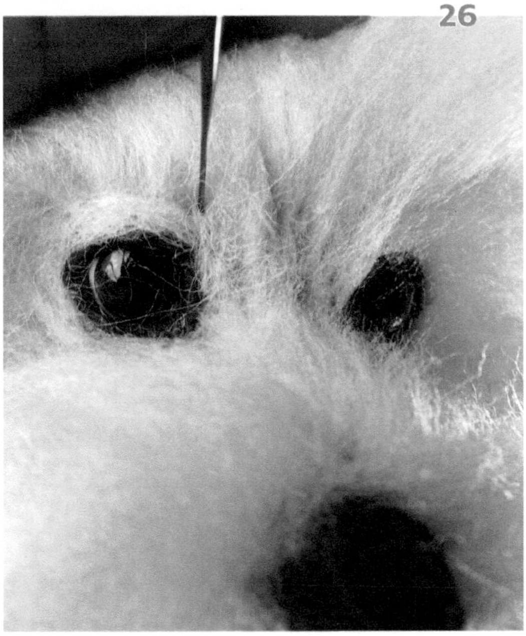

26

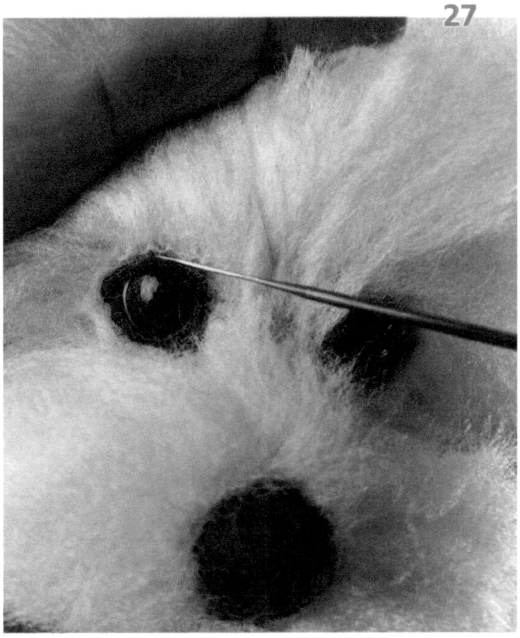

27

28

part at the top of each ear. Give the face a little trim so that the eyes are easily accessed.

Step 14
26-28

Glue the final eyes in place and leave to dry. Ensure that the eyes are clear of fuzziness, ready for the eyelids. Clip away any stray fur and make sure there is nothing on the eyes that could become stuck to them. Ensure the eye is completely clean and free from wool, as even one stray fibre will show when the eyes are glossed.

Use the same method as for the Chihuahua to make the eyelids, but roll the black Silk Clay slightly thinner – just over 1mm (0.39in) in thickness as these are smaller eyes. Working on one eye at a time, paint Mod Podge Gloss around the inside edge of the eye, particularly into the corners, to ensure the clay sticks and holds in place. Roll two lengths, one slightly longer: just over 2cm (0.78in) for the upper eyelid and one slightly shorter at just over 1.5cm (0.59in) for the lower eyelid. Place the lower eyelid first, using small clay modelling tools. Mould the clay into place using the horseshoe-shape ended tool, leaving a smooth, clean finish. Use the pointed tool to indent the corners of each eye.

Add the upper eyelid in the same way. Trim excess clay from the corners whilst still soft, and smooth over.

When the clay is dry, finish adding fur around the eyes (you might have to add a little more core up to the edges of the eyelids, into which you can then attach more long fur). Image 28 shows one eye surround – the right side – almost done, with the other still requiring attention. The end result should be a natural transition from partly-covered Silk Clay eyelid to surrounding fur.

Step 15
29-32

For the black Poodle, starting at the base attach shorter, finer lengths of fur around half of the tail, then longer lengths (around 10cm (3.93in)) to the remaining half.

For the white Poodle attach lengths of 10cm (3.93in) over the whole tail and clip to shape.

With all of the fur attached (except in the neck area so that the sculpture can be handled without flattening the wool), an initial clipping comes next. Don't try and do the clipping all in one go: several stages will be required. Start with a light trim, then assess the shape, trim again, assess the shape, trim again, etc. After each trim, use the 3-needle tool to arrange and fluff the coat, ready for the next trim. Don't 'comb' the fur, but gently tease it into place and fluff it up.

There is no specific place to start clipping the Poodle, though I like to start with the paws to ensure I have them clipped evenly, and check that they are centrally placed

29

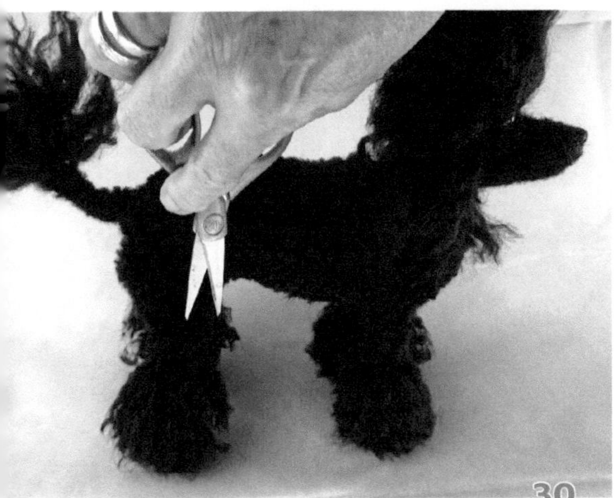
30

31

32

in the surrounding fur which will help achieve a nice even clip down the leg.

When I have done the paws, I usually start around the body, fluffing up the fur after each trim. I leave the finer clipping of the face until last. Always trim in the direction of fur growth, as this will ensure a nice soft edge to the cut. Note also that the fur along the top of the muzzle is a lot shorter than on the rest of the face.

For the black Poodle, I have cut the muzzle fur very short and left a long top knot, which can be tied with a bow.

TIP

It's always better to trim too little than too much. You can't put back what has been trimmed off, and the only option is to pull out all of the fur affected and reattach more to trim again. Keep track of where your sculpture is under all that fur,

33

34

35

too, as it is easy to make an uneven cut around the body. Clip over a couple of days and take photos of the sculpture as you do to get a different perspective of your work. Often faults can show up in photos, or even simply looking at it in the mirror. You might find it helpful to pin each paw onto a felting sponge to hold it still whilst you clip

Step 16
33-35

With the Poodle trimmed, add final details around the eyes and nose. If the Silk Clay method was used to create the nose, for the white Poodle add a light covering of fur to the back part of the top of the nose,

36

38

37

where hair grows on the edge. Apply a thin layer of Mod Podge Silk, cut a very fine length of wool and hold with tweezers, as shown. Before adding this to the nose, trim level underneath the tweezers to make a nice even length. Place on the back of the top of the nose, slightly to one side, and gently pat into place.

Do the same for the other side of the nose and leave to dry. Extra fur can be added around the rest of the nose and eyelids, but this might not be needed.

Step 17
36-38

When the final fur attachments around the nose are dry, trim to length.

Colour around the nose, muzzle and eyes with GB9, applying this VERY gently so as not to overdo the colour. Unwanted colouring can be part rectified by brushing over with some lighter-coloured Pan Pastel.

39

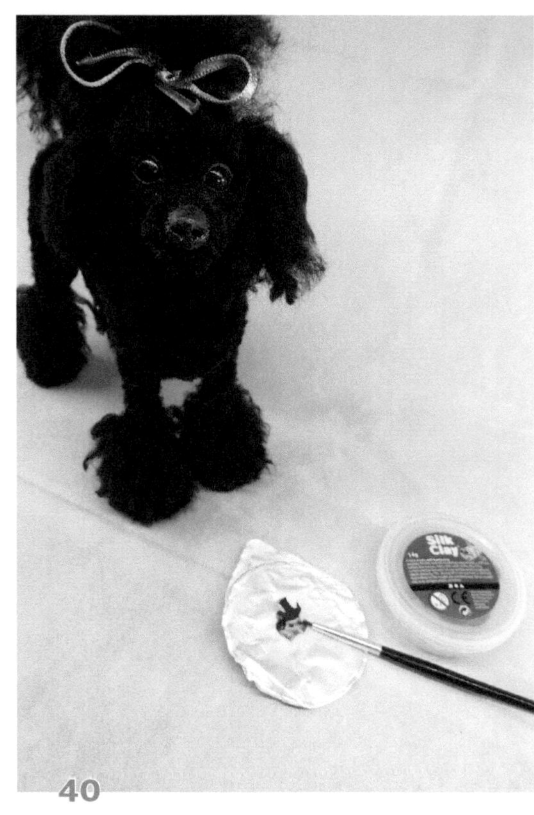

40

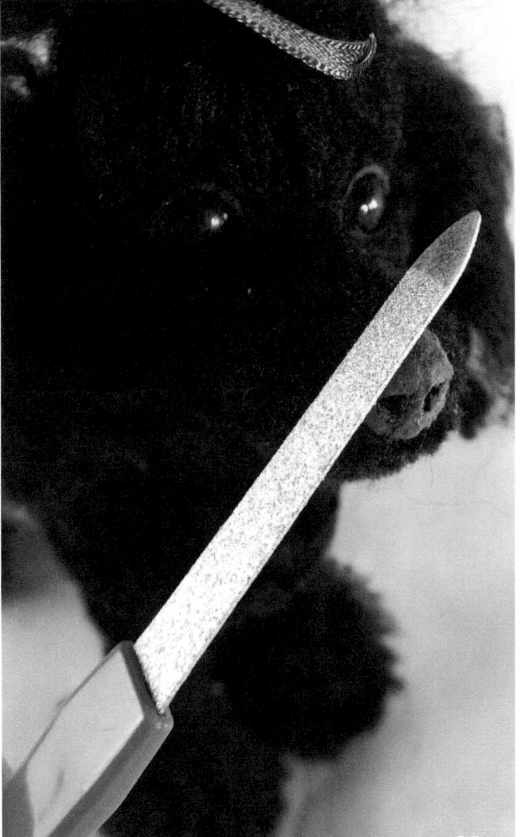
41

Step 18
39-41

If the nose has been created using Silk Clay, you might have found that the first sculpting and moulding didn't go to plan. Freehand noses aren't the easiest of things to sculpt. Silk Clay is water-based, you needn't worry too much. Place a small amount of Silk Clay on a piece of foil and use a small brush to mix with a drop of water, so that the Silk Clay becomes a lot softer and gooey. Use the brush to apply it to the muzzle and, as it starts to set, continue to mould and play with textures.

If you find you need more time, simply wet the nose again. Applying the clay with a brush, rather than a firmer tool. seems to work well. When dry use a nail file to gently smooth any rough area, then colour with a black Spectrum Noir pen. Seal with Mod Podge Satin and you're done.

Making the collar and lead is described in the, Accessories chapter.

HOW TO PREPARE & BLEND MERINO WOOL

I have heard many felters mention how difficult to handle Merino wool tops is, especially for long coats, and I too found it difficult at first. The end result can appear very flat and featureless, and make a sculpture look awful, but I didn't give up, and found that, with a little know-how, preparation and texturing, sculptures can be transformed. The really magical quality of Merino is its ability to blend, and given the huge range of dyed colours available, the colour palette is huge. I haven't encountered a single dog coat colour that cannot be achieved with Merino tops.

Preparation

You will need lengths of wool and two small, metal-toothed carders, or small metal dog brushes (I find larger carders very difficult to manage).

1

Merino wool is supplied as a ball or wrapped, and unravels into one long length, the width of which is usually the same wherever it is purchased. For blending, the wool should be cut into lengths: if using the felt down the centre of the length attachment method, double the finished fur length, plus 1cm (0.39in), is what is required; if using the top of the length attachment method, the length plus 1cm is what's needed (in both cases, the extra 1cm is to allow for attachment as well as allowing for trimming.

So, for example, using down the centre attachment for a coat length of 2cm (0.78in), cut 5cm (1.96in) lengths. Using top attachment for a coat length of 3cm (1.18in), cut 4cm (1.57in) lengths. Be aware, however, that Merino isn't very suitable for coat lengths of more than 4cm because the fibres are in general, not a lot longer than this.

With small carders and the cut Merino lengths it's easy to card a length at a time to separate it, or, if blending colours, split it in half and combine with half a length of the other colour. Carding/blending more than this with small carders will be very difficult.

To prepare (card) the Merino colours, place one length on a carding brush, and gently brush over it with the other brush so that the fibres separate and eventually transfer onto the second brush.

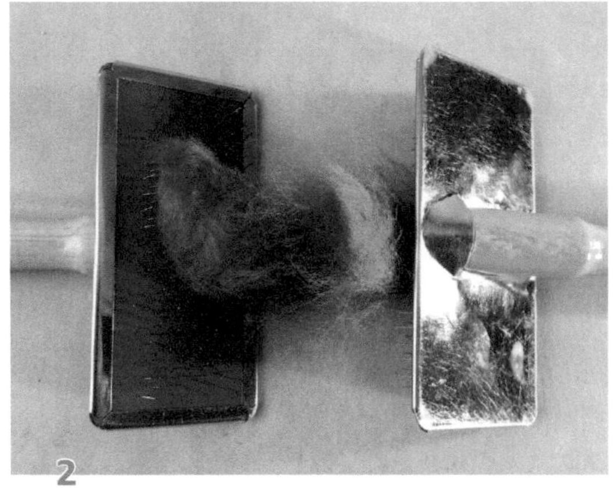
2

3

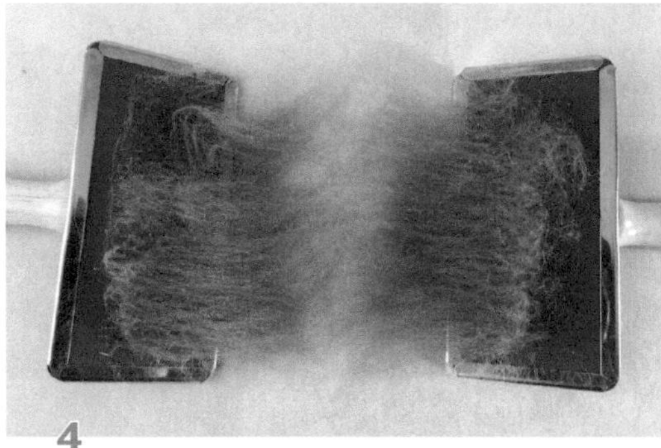
4

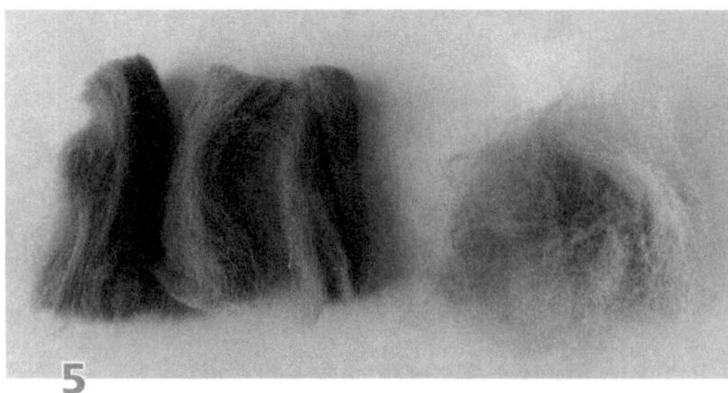
5

Don't be rough with this; take your time and do it gently, otherwise the fibres may break into smaller lengths and become tangled. Once all of the fibres have been transferred to the second brush, swap the brushes and repeat this step.

You might need to do this two or three times, until all the fibres are loose and fluffed, and you cannot see any cut edges. This conditioned wool is now ready to use.

Blending

To blend two colours in a 50:50 mix, split the prepared Merino into two equal sections and place both on one brush.

Card this as you would a single colour, but now and then taking the carded wool from the second brush and placing it back on the first.

Repeat until the colours are blended to your liking.

You may well have to do this five or six times to achieve a good blend, but less often with practice. Of course, you could prep each colour separately, then lay one on top the other on the brush and blend. With experience, you will find a way that suits you.

Image 9 shows the level of detail that can be achieved by Merino blending with the German Shepherd sable coat.

Experiment with different ratios of colours: you can even blend the blends, making the range of colours and hues limitless!

TIP

When brushing and mixing, be sure to brush one colour over another to help the mix. For example, if you lay the colours side-by-side on the first brush they won't mix well: place the colours one on top of the other

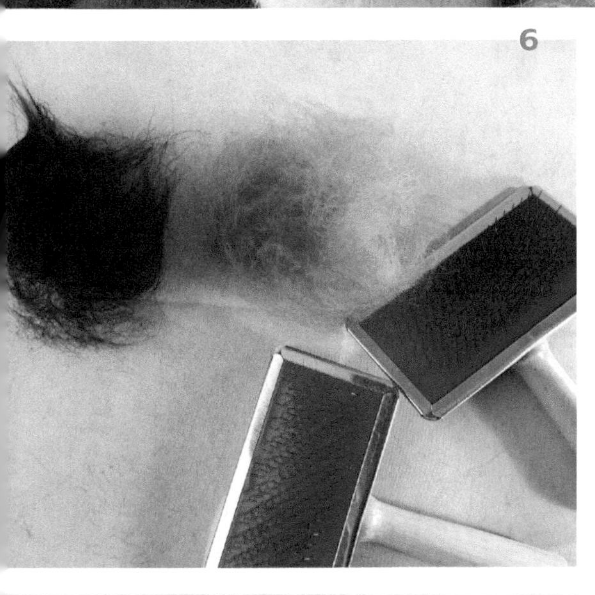

6

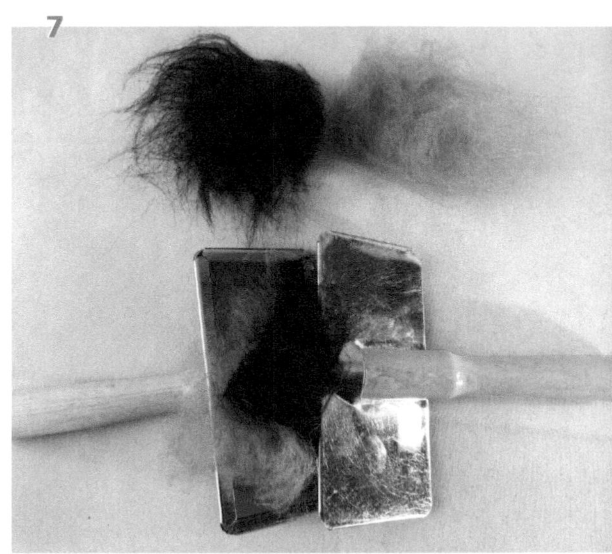

7

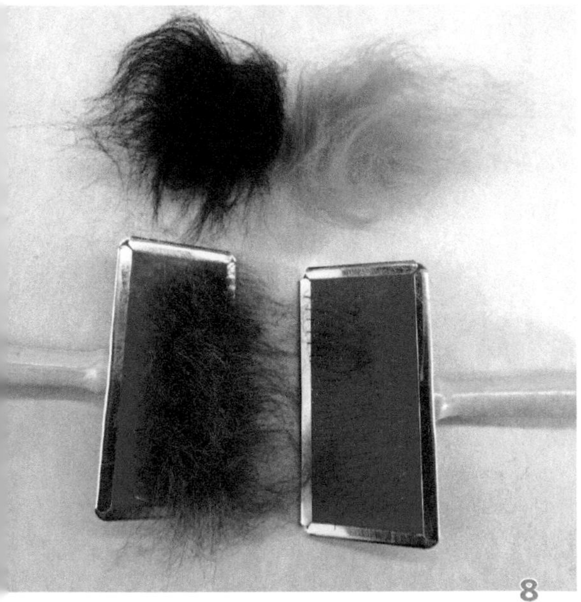

8

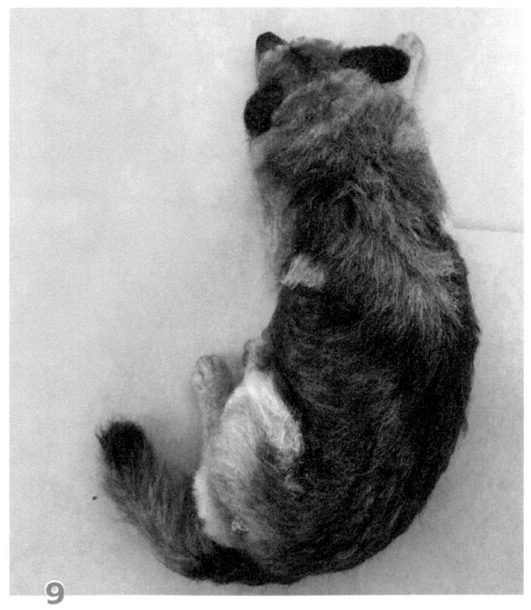

9

ACCESSORIES

Accessories – polymer clay extras – can accompany and greatly enhance your sculptures, adding realism and interest.

Here, I describe how to make a collar and lead, and a bowl of food with a bone.

Materials & tools needed for bowl of food/bone

- Polymer clay colours of your choice for the bowl and the food: I have used Terracotta and Sahara
- FIMO liquid
- Scalpel or craft blade
- Rolling pin
- Ball and dotting tool
- 5cm (1.96in) circle cutter
- A hard work surface or durable tile
- Tinfoil
- Awl
- Mod Podge, Satin, or Gloss and Matt, to seal the finished item
- Pastel set
- Fine brush for painting & a slightly wider brush for applying pastels
- Toothbrush
- Small sanding block
- Acrylic paints to finalise the bowl
- Tape measure/ruler
- Petroleum jelly & hammer (in case clay is very dry)

Note: If the clay is really hard, begin by tapping it flat with a clean hammer on a hard, unbreakable surface. Rub a little petroleum jelly over half the surface, fold over and tap again.

Repeat the exercise, adding jelly between the layers as needed, and the clay will eventually become supple again.

The bowl

Step 1

1

With a rolling pin roll out the colour clay of your choice to about 2-3mm (0.08-0.11in) thickness. Cut a 5mm (1.96in) circle with the cutter to make the bowl base, place on a flat, heatproof surface and bake for ten minutes at 130°C (266°F). Allow to cool.

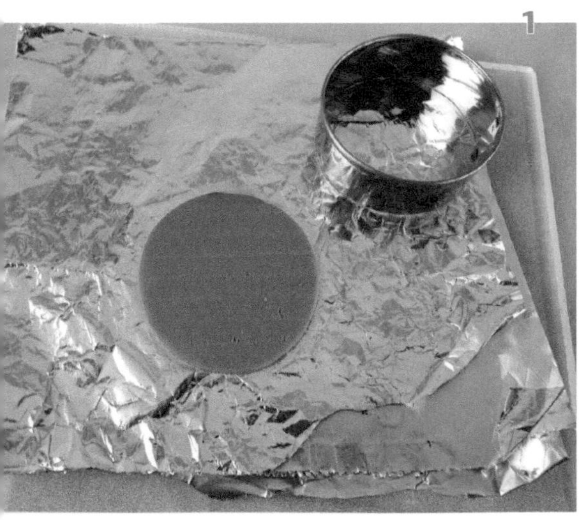
1

Step 2

2-4

To make the sides of the bowl, roll out more clay to the same thickness as for the bowl base, and long enough to go completely around the edge of the bowl (roughly 9cm (3.54in)). Use a scalpel or craft blade to cut a length of clay 9cm (3.54in) long by 1.5cm (0.59in) wide, and wrap around the base of the bowl (easier

2
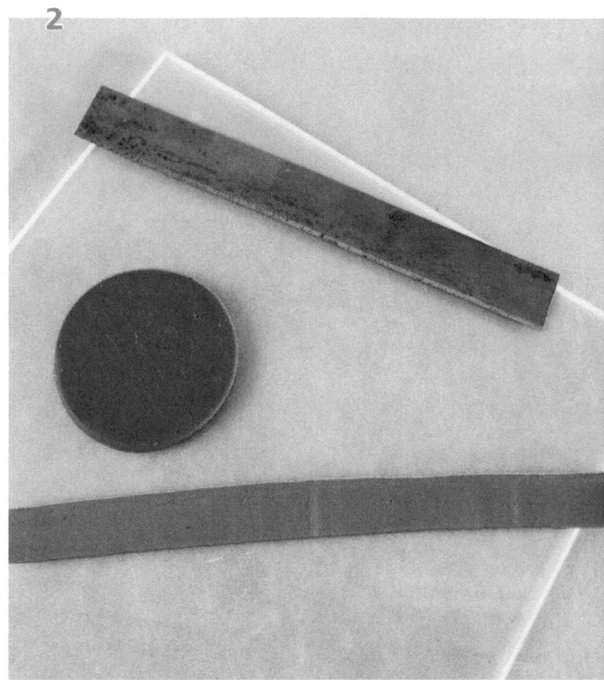

3

if you place on the surface outside the circle, rather than trying to balance it on top of the circle), and trim to fit. Smooth the join and gently press the sides into the bottom, but not so hard that it becomes misshaped. Run a thin line of FIMO liquid along the inside join. Bake again for ten

4

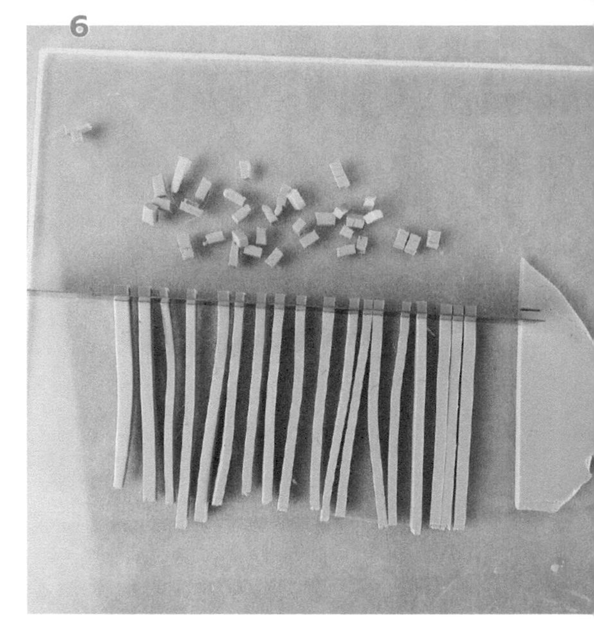
6

minutes at 130°C (266°F. Allow to cool.

The food

Step 3

5, 6

Roll out a thin square of the second clay colour to around a 2mm (0.08in) thickness. You could use brown, but I have used Sahara. Using the craft blade or scalpel, cut into thin strips, then cut the strips into small squares.

Step 4

7, 8

With scrunched tinfoil texture the surface of the little squarcs. If you have used a light-coloured clay, colour with brown pastel.

Use the scalpel to scrape dark brown pastel dust over the clay, and, with a brush, coat the clay pieces with the scraped pastel.

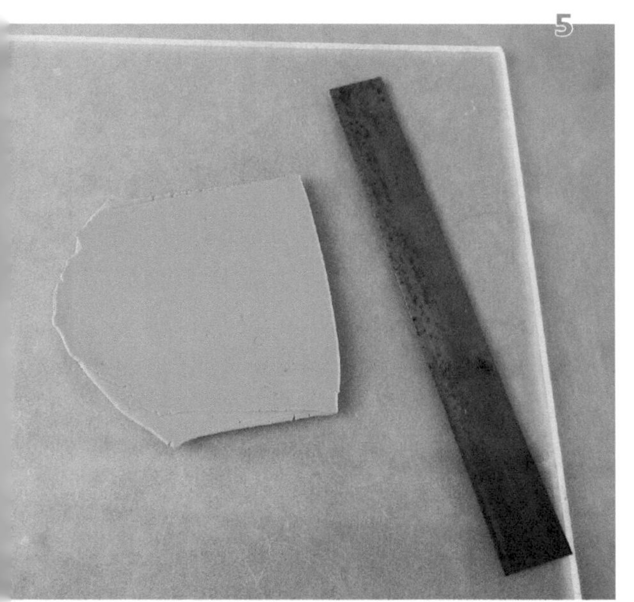
5

7

Step 5
9-11

To add gravy to the 'meat chunks,' combine brown pastel dust with FIMO liquid and

mix well, then coat the chunks with this. Place in the bowl, arrange and bake for ten minutes at temperature previously given. Allow to cool.

Step 6
12, 13

Sand the finished bowl to make the edges and sides smoother. Wipe away the dust with a damp cloth, then either paint the

12

13

14

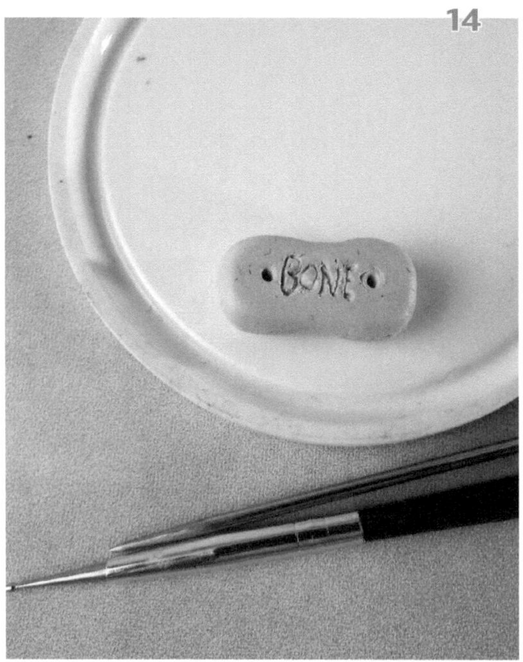

15

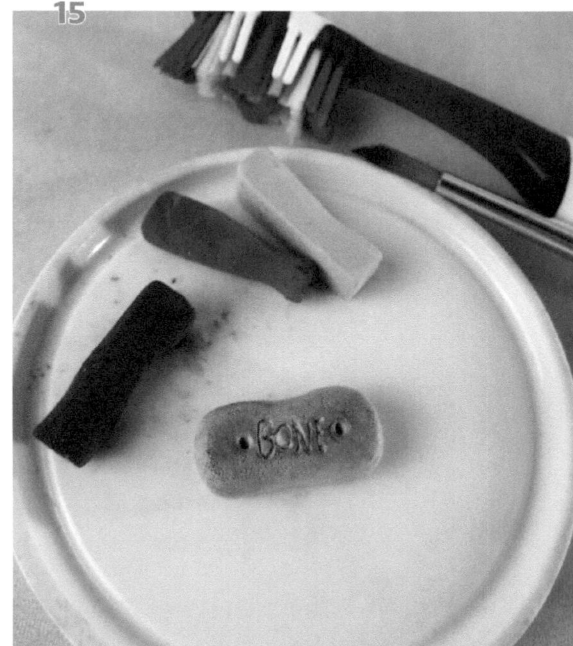

16

outside of the bowl a different colour to the inside, or simply give it a coating of Mod Podge of your choice: Matt, Satin or Gloss. Allow to dry and you're done!

Biscuit bone

Step 1

14-16

To make a little bone, take an amount of Sahara clay and roll out into a bone shape. Use the awl to mark some holes and give a little texture, then use a toothbrush to stipple the surface for additional texture.

Now colour, first with light brown pastel (with a small paintbrush first rub on the pastel and then onto the bone); then apply an outer edge covering of mid brown pastel to give the bone the appearance of having been baked.

Finally, lightly apply detail with dark brown pastel. Bake for ten minutes at 130°C. (266°F) When cool, apply a coating of Mod Podge Matt and you're done!

Materials & tools for collar & lead

- 60cm (24in) length of leather, 1mm (0.04in) thick and 5mm (0.19in) wide; any colour
- Open jump rings (for jewellery-making) 1 x 7mm (0.04 x 0.27in)and 2 x 5mm (0.07 x 0.19in)
- 0.8mm (0.03in) gauge craft wire
- 4 x 3mm (0.15 x 0.11in) single cap rivets
- 2.5cm (0.09in) swivel Lobster spring clip
- Diamante crystals (self-adhesive, nail art-type)
- Tweezers
- Hammer
- 1.5mm (0.06in) leather hole punch
- Hand setter for punching rivets (and small block of wood to work on)
- Pliers (needle-nose)
- Wire cutters
- Wire crimper
- Tape measure/ruler

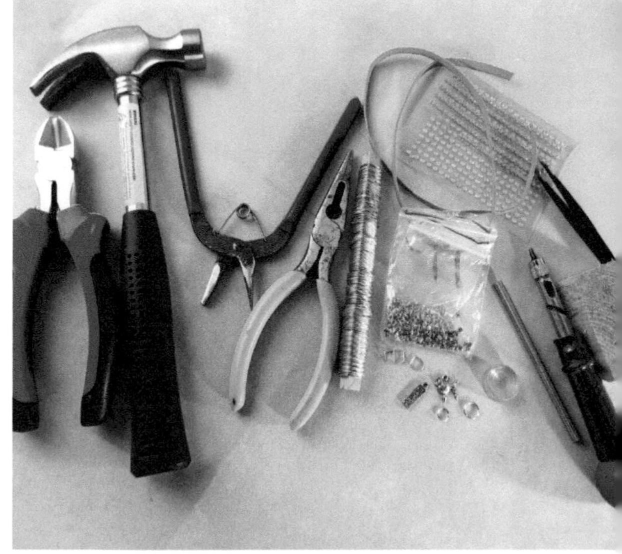

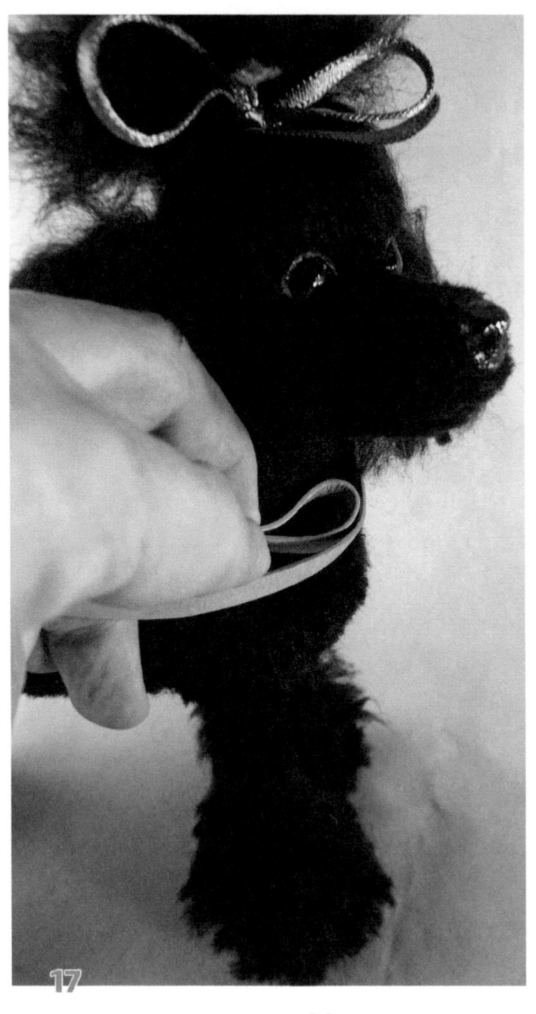
17

Step 1
17

Measure the leather needed for the collar by first folding over one end of the piece by 3cm (1.18in). Wrap the leather around the dog's neck and, with one finger inside the wrap to provide clearance, overlap the other end over the fold by 3cm (1.18in) and cut.

The buckle and rivets will be located along the first 3mm fold.

This collar is intended for the Poodle, and, depending on neck thickness, will be around 23cm (9.05in) in length.

Step 2
18

To make the buckle, cut a length of wire of about 6cm (2.36in). I have listed the bends required to make it easier to follow the steps (essentially, you need a square figure of eight). Using a wire crimper make inward bends at 90° angles –

- First bend at 5mm (0.19in) (this first

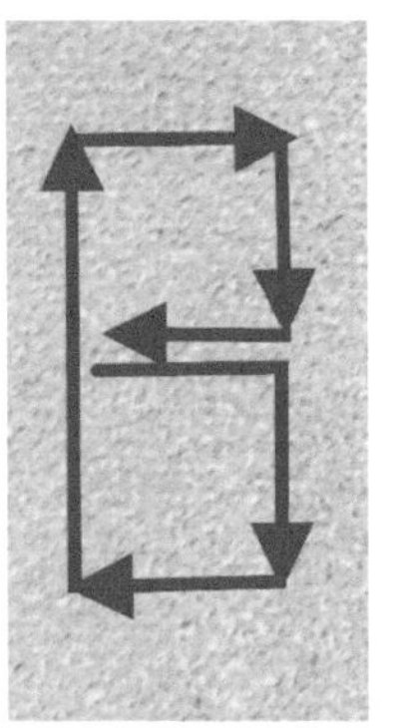

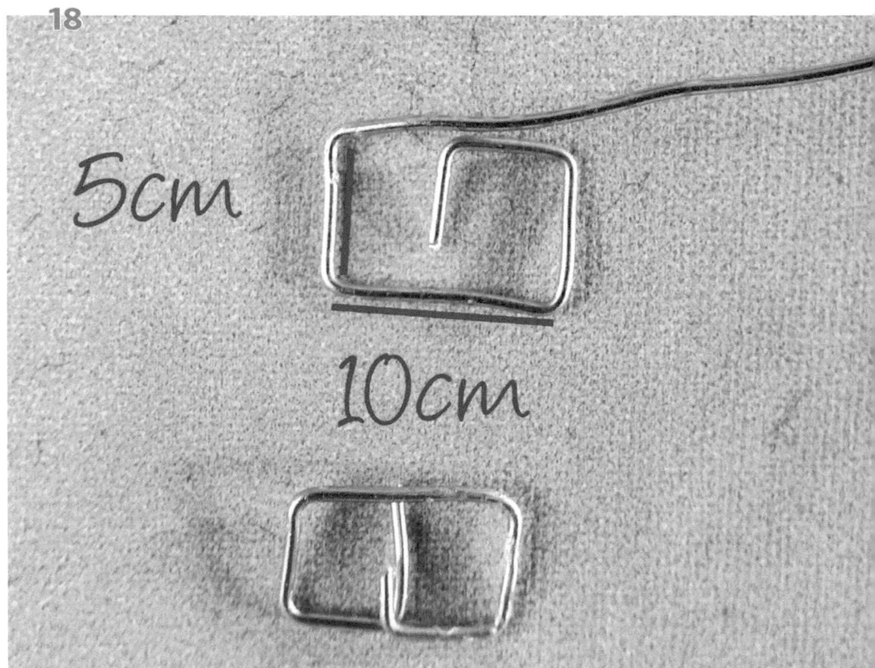

18

length is the centre of the buckle, and will not be seen under the leather)

- Second bend at 5mm (0.19in) (this is the first side of the buckle)
- Third bend at 5mm (0.19in) (this measurement must be 5mm on the inside to accept the 5mm (0.19in) leather and will be one end of the buckle. Check that the leather fits before moving on)
- Fourth bend at 10mm (0.38in) (one complete side done)
- Fifth bend at 5mm (0.19in) (again, ensure the leather fits inside as this is the other end of the buckle)
- Last bend at 5mm (0.19in) (the last piece going into the centre to finish off)
- Trim the last bend to fit inside the buckle

Step 3

Bend both ends of the finished buckle so that they are slightly higher than the centre piece when laid flat. This will make threading the other end of the collar through the buckle a lot easier once fitted.

Step 4
19

With the buckle threaded onto one end of the collar, fold back 3mm (1.18in) of leather, then, 5mm (0.19in) from the buckle, mark where the first rivet will be located, with the second rivet at 7mm (0.27in) from the this.

The jump ring will be located between the two rivets, onto which the lead will attach.

Step 5
20, 21

Lay the leather flat and punch the holes where marked, then refold the leather and mark corresponding points on the leather folded under the top piece. Unfold the leather and punch the holes where

19

20

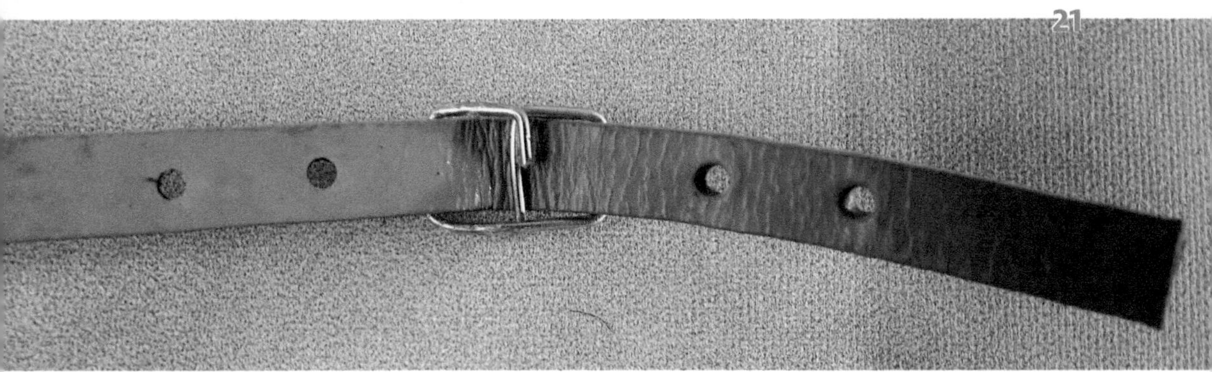

21

marked, taking care to punch centrally on the leather.

Step 6
22, 23

With the buckle in place and the holes punched, fit the first rivet (the one closest to the buckle), making sure that the top of the rivet is on the right side of the collar, not the inside, and that both lengths of leather are aligned one with the other. They cannot be moved once the rivet has been fixed.

Step 7
24

Thread the 7mm (0.27in) jump ring onto the collar (use the pliers to flatten where the ring joins to make it sit better on the collar). With the jump ring in place, fix the second rivet, which will hold the ring (it's easier to fit this ring now rather than later).

Step 8
25

Punch four or five more holes equidistant roughly 10cm (3.93in) from the second rivet. This will make the collar look more realistic.

Step 9
26

For effect, stick Diamante crystals to the collar. If you'd like to add a little charm to the collar, firstly attach this to the other 5mm jump ring, and then attach the jump ring to the collar as previously.

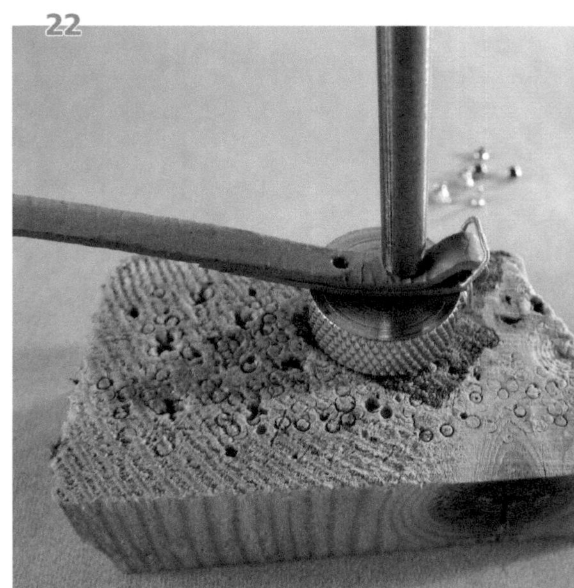
22

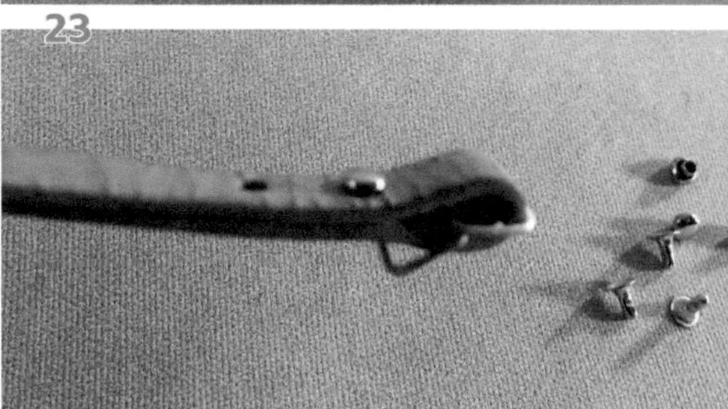
23

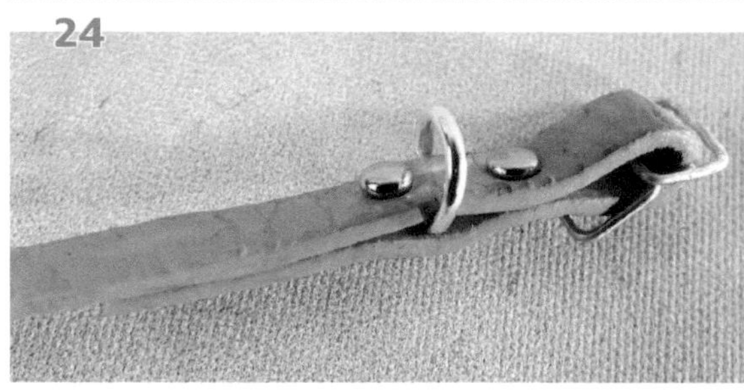
24

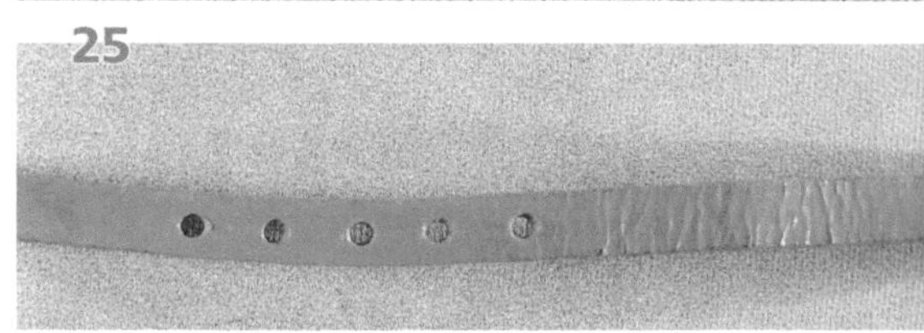
25

The lead

Step 10
27-29

Measure and cut roughly 30cm (11.81in) from the remaining leather. Fit the 5mm (0.19in) jump ring onto the end of the Lobster clip with the pliers. Thread one end of the leather through the ring, and fold over the end enough to place another rivet, making a loop.

Do the same with the leather at the other

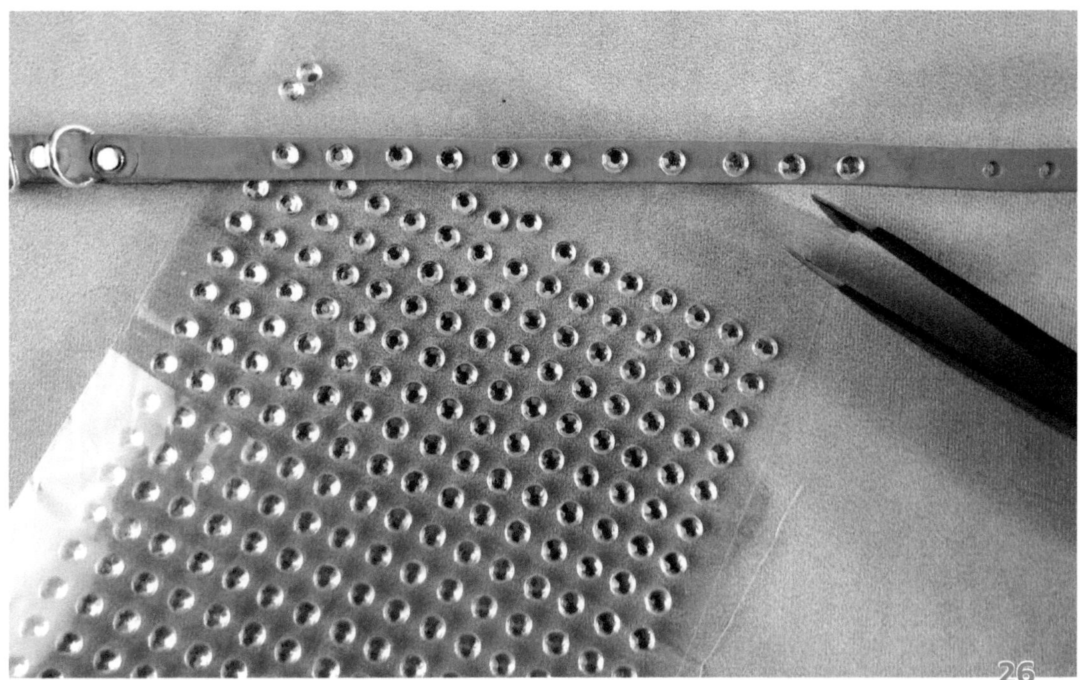

26

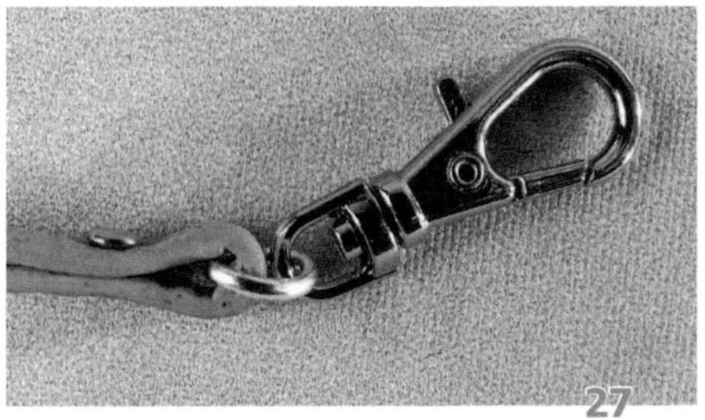

27

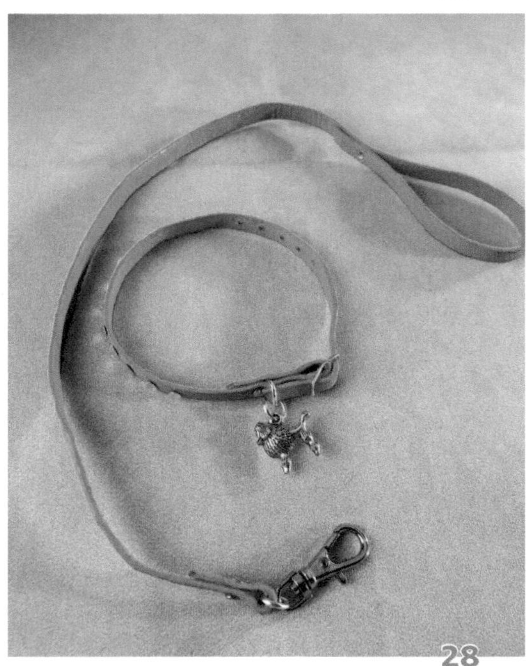

28

29

end, only this time make a bigger loop to represent the lead's handle.

Put the collar on the dog, attach the lead and you're done!

TROUBLESHOOTING

Many people are afraid of making mistakes, but making mistakes will always teach us something, even if it is only not to do it again, and in the process it might also suggest another way of doing something, or an idea not yet thought of.

It was making a mistake that led me to develop and make my realistic eyes. I had a mixture of acrylic beads – a job-lot – and was making a brown dog. In order to see the eye socket shape easily I placed white spacer beads in the sockets, so that the eye shape was a lot easier to see. I used alcohol pens to colour detail on my sculptures, particularly around the eyes before adding Silk Clay eyelids. On this particular occasion, I removed the white spacer beads, marked the inside of the eye with an alcohol pen, and popped the white beads straight back into their sockets.

When I removed them to replace them with glass beads, I noticed that the alcohol pen had coloured the white bead really strongly! It was a eureka moment and I began looking at ways to colour the white beads to make them into eyes.

Making a perfect circle freehand was impossible ... perhaps a plastic circle template (the protractor type used in mathematics) would work? And it did! The next problem was glossing the eyes. I discovered that anything other than water-based glaze simply mixed with the alcohol inks and made them run, but using a water-based glaze/gloss this didn't happen.

A particular problem felters encounter is the dreaded shrinkage. This is when a particularly intricate bit is worked on for a long time, and the wool becomes increasingly compacted, making the sculpture smaller. This problem is particularly troublesome on muzzles.

Image 1 shows a commission I did of a little terrier. The customer was unhappy with the muzzle, which she said wasn't long enough. Having already done a lot of work on this dog, I didn't fancy starting over again ... I had to come up with a remedy that resolved the problem without leaving any trace.

I decided to cut into the muzzle at an angle (rather than straight), which would help when the muzzle was felted back together as the edges would slightly overlap, and could be easily merged and smoothed. I cut a V-shape almost to the wire, and gently extended the end of the muzzle without detaching it (image 2).

I then packed the gap and covered it with the same colour wool. Cutting it straight would have made rejoining the edges difficult, as it tends to cause a 'step,' which is hard to disguise. With the muzzle packed and covered with wool, the difference in length is clearly visible (image 3, overleaf), but the join isn't ...

... and the customer was very happy with the result (image 4, overleaf).

I sometimes find that the chest of my sculpture is narrower than I would like, but, with all of the top coat already added, pulling it out in order to build up the chest would be very time-consuming Image 5).

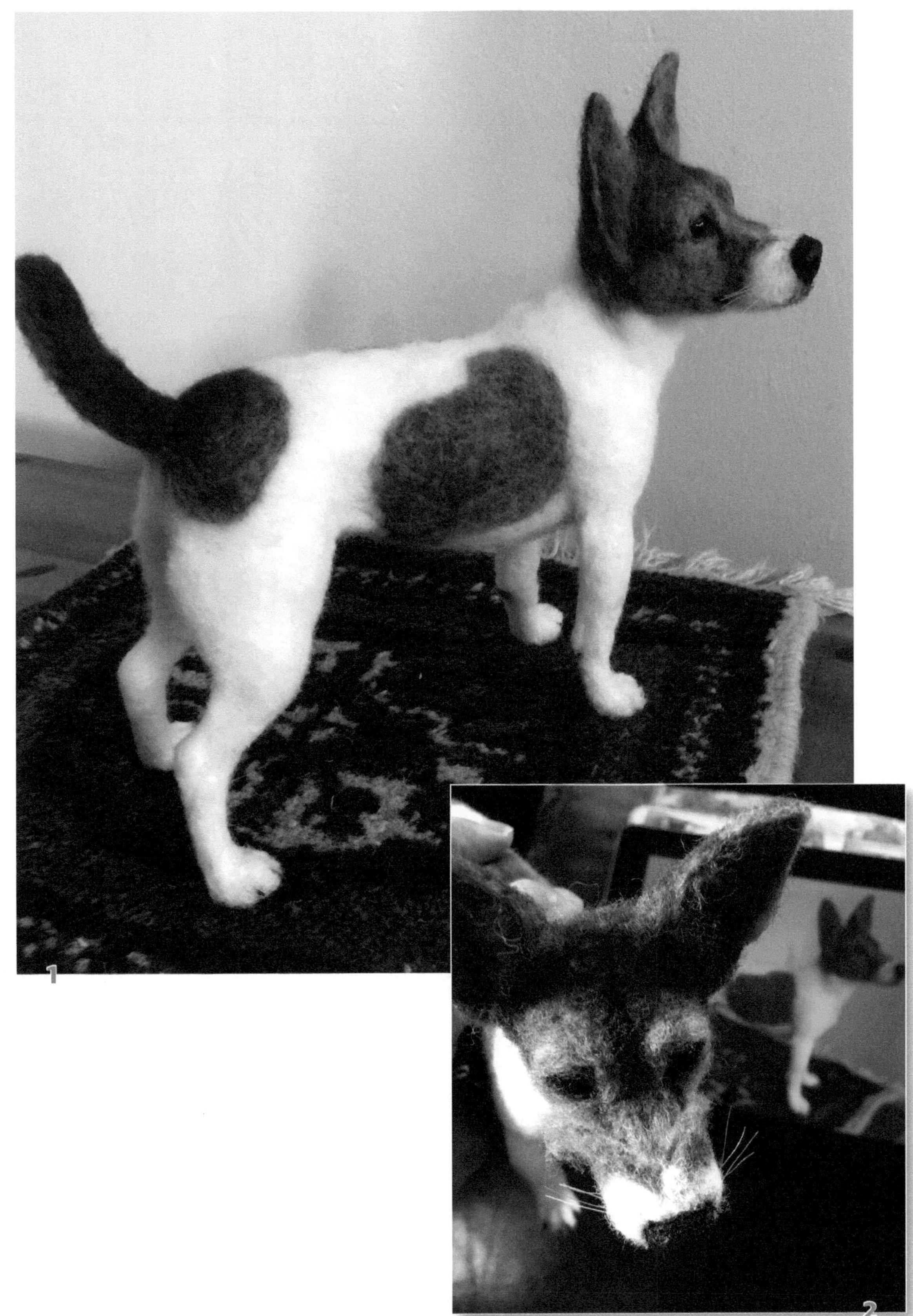
1
2

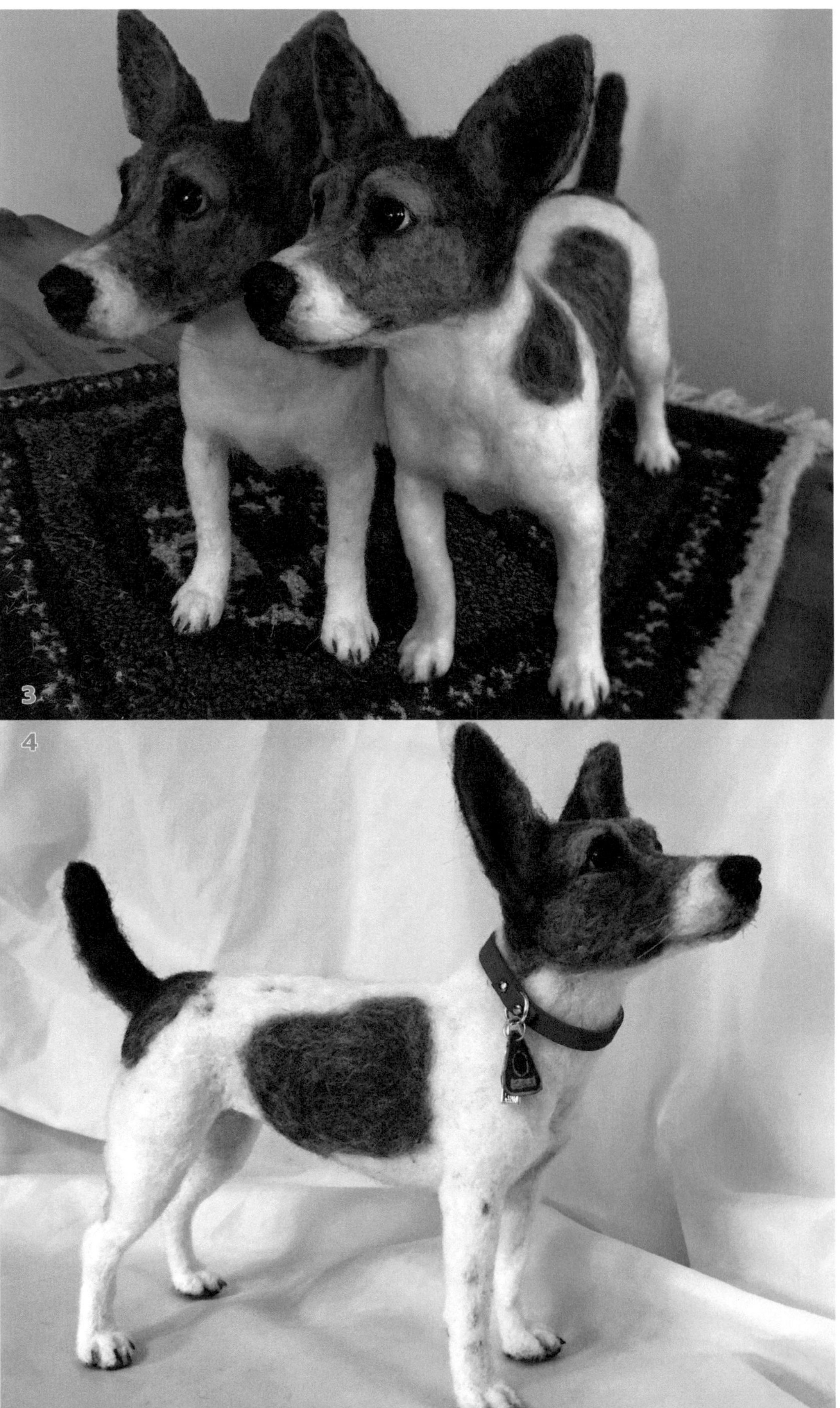
3
4

5

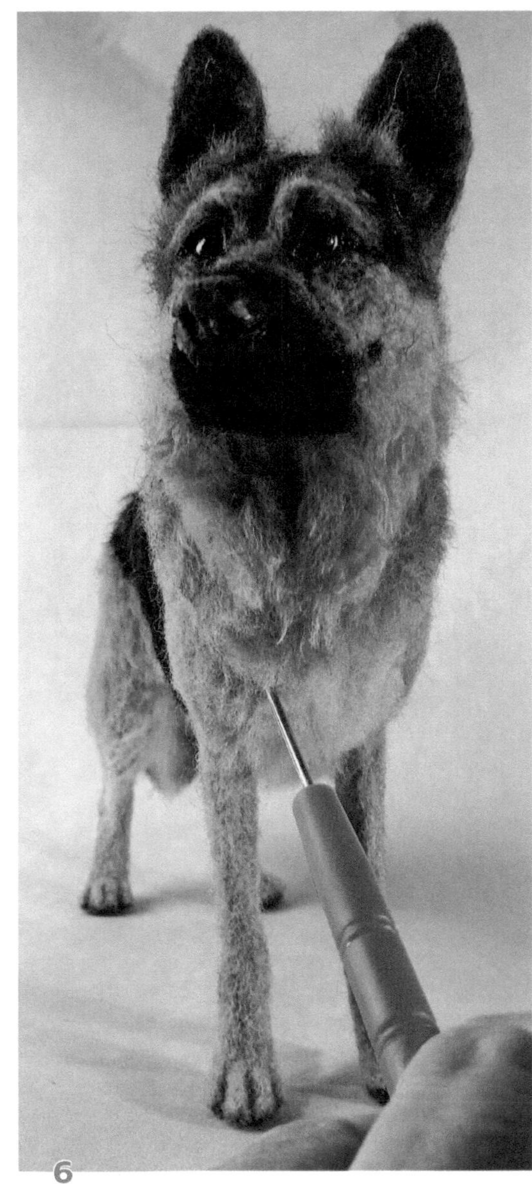
6

I first try using an awl to poke into the front of the chest along the shoulders, and push out the sides of the shoulders to broaden the chest (Image 6).

Often, this can be enough to salvage the situation, but, if it isn't, a more drastic remedy is required. Cutting into the chest from the front, following the same path as the awl method, and in alongside the shoulder/chest on both sides (two separate cuts) makes it possible to 'stuff' core wool into the cavity to achieve a broader chest. Don't cut too close to the 'skin,' and make the cavity slightly larger than needed to allow the stuffing to lay evenly up to the cut edges. Do this slowly and carefully, and ensure the wool is packed evenly within the cavity (any large lumps will show). You don't even need to felt the stuffing in place, but simply close up the cuts. Felt over the cuts and re-apply top coat to cover them.

Another issue can be over-colouring the wool when finishing off. Colouring can

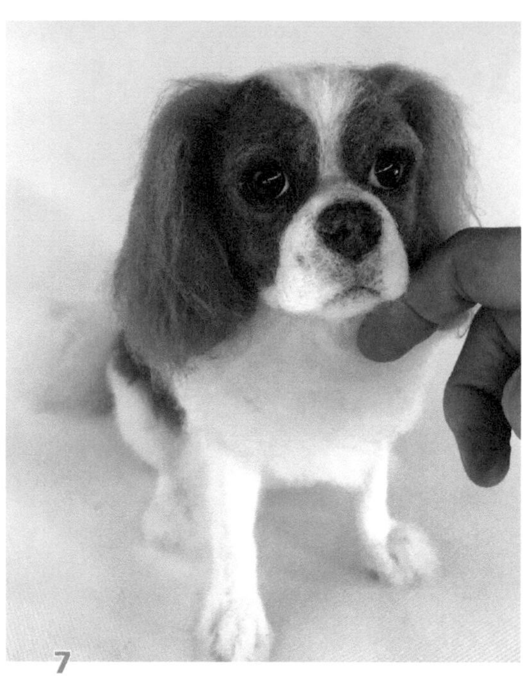
7

make all the difference between a very flat, dull appearance, to a much more realistic one (image 7).

Highlights can be a little overpowering, especially if done in poor lighting. Those in image 8 were made by lightly brushing off-white acrylic paint into the wool.

It's possible to tone down highlights, though, by either going over them with a darker colour highlight of acrylic paint, or a thin covering of the coat colour wool. Image 9 shows how toning down has considerably improved the left side. In hindsight, it would have been far better to add a colour somewhere between off-white and the coat colour of the dog in the first place; just enough to give a highlight.

8

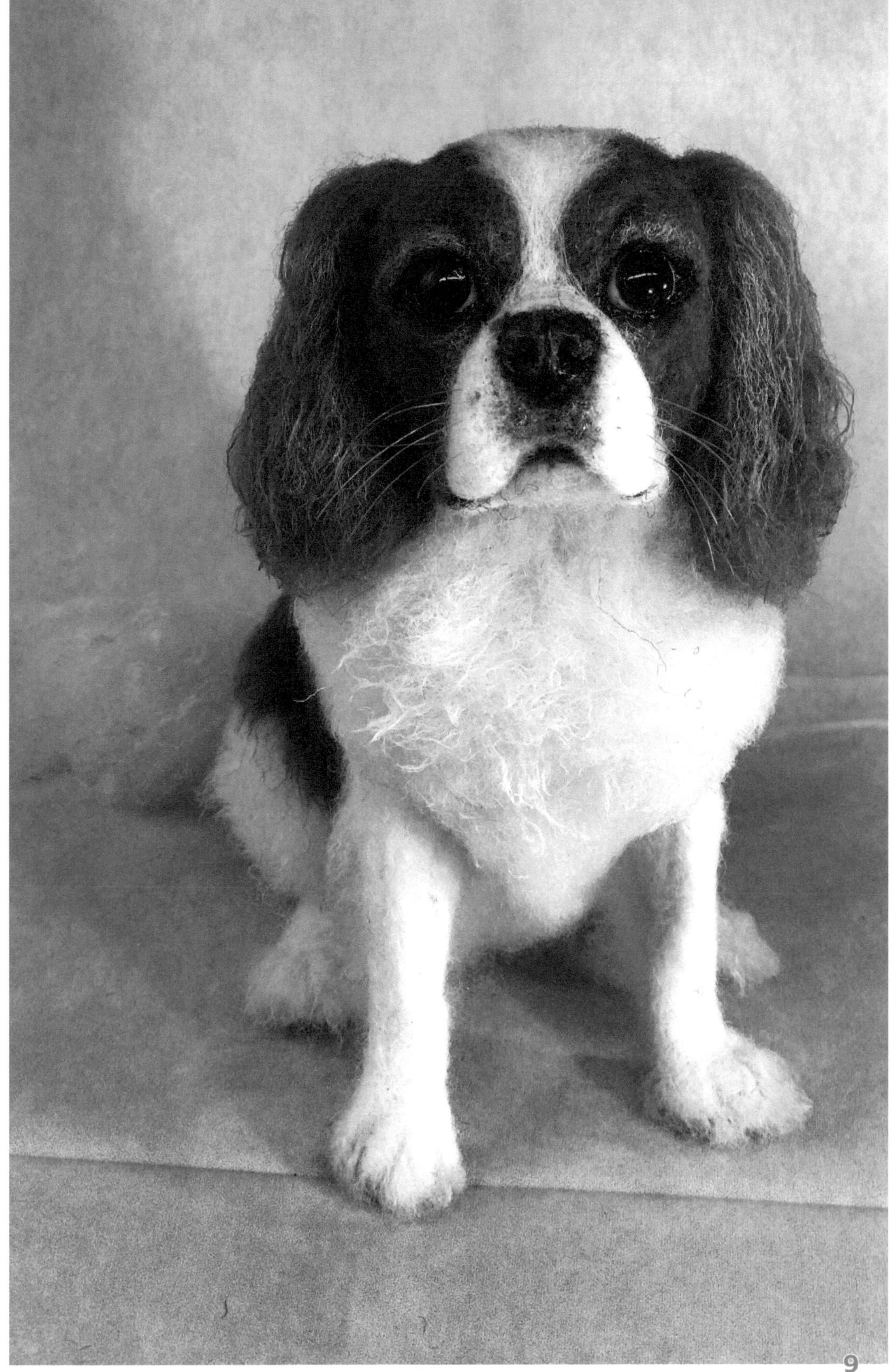

GLOSSARY & SUPPLIERS

Alcohol pens
A dye in pen form that can be used to colour a range of materials, including wool and acrylic beads – even clay

Armature
A wire frame that offers support and guidance of size and proportions throughout the creation process

Awl
A thin, metal pointed tool with a handle, for use with delicate tiny-sized items

Cabochon
A lens that is circular, crystal clear, and with two sides – one convex the other flat – perfect for making eyes, when a printed eye is glued to the underside to show through the lens

Carders
Two flat, metal-toothed brushes, used to card 'brush' wool to either make it fluffy or to blend colours. Always used in pairs

Core wool (batts US)
Fleece that has been cleaned of any debris, washed to remove the lanolin, and carded (brushed) to make it fluffy and uniform. Core can also be processed into slivers, long lengths, that can be used in the same way as normal core

Crimp
To use pliers to tightly bend back the armature wire over wrapped wool to hold the wool in place

Diamond Glaze
A clear, 3-dimensional medium used to gloss eye beads. As it is water based, it doesn't mix with the alcohol colours it is being used to seal

Felt down
To use felting needles to needle felt, and so compact the wool into shape

Felting brush
A square, long-bristled brush, used bristles up to achieve flat felting. Usually used in conjunction with a multi-needle (sprung-type)

Glossy Accents
A clear, 3-dimensional medium, used to gloss eye beads

Jump ring
Used in jewellery making, a ring that can be easily opened, connected to something else and pinched closed again

Liquid FIMO
A liquid form of polymer clay, mostly used to glue clay to clay, especially after part-baking/baking and adding another dimension to the project

Lobster clip
A clip with a hinged opening (like on the end of a dog lead) which can be used to attach to a ring

Mod Podge
A large range of water-based decoupage

mediums: an all-in-one glue, sealer and finish for use in a range of crafting applications, including needle felting

Multi-needles

- Open multi-needle tool: a needle holder that can hold any number of needles, usually arranged in a circle
- Sprung multi-needle tool: another multi-needle holder that can hold 5 or 7 needles encased in a sprung shield
- 3-needle tool: one of my favourite tools, this is a 3-needle holder; the needles arranged in a row

Pan Pastels

Super soft pastels in a 'pan' which can be applied with a paint brush to add colour detailing to a sculpture. Pigments are very strong and long-lasting

Pins

Two types of pins are used in this book: ordinary, round-headed sewing pins for indicating nostrils , and the longer, thicker, large-headed pins, also called hat pins, which are essential for ear placement so that they are level and in the right pose, before they are felted onto the sculpture

Polymer clay

A type of clay that can be moulded into any shape, then baked to 'cure' it (make it hard). The most popular brand of polymer clay is FIMO

PVA Glue

A white, clear-drying craft glue, adequate for most needle felting needs, used to glue eyes in place, nails into toes, noses onto muzzles, and wool onto clay

Reverse-felt

Using a needle that has barbs in the opposite direction to normal felting needles, to either blend layers of different coloured wools, or to fluff the surface of felted wool

Rubber-tipped clay tools

A range of tools with soft rubber tips, which allow a more gentle touch with clay. Particularly useful for applying Silk Clay eyelids

Sculpting tools

A range of metal or rubber-tipped tools, used to shape and texture clay

Silk Clay

A self-hardening clay that dries at room temperature to a soft, rubber-like texture

Spacer beads

My own term: any bead that can be used to form a perfect cavity for coloured acrylic eye beads

Spectrum Noir Pens

A make of alcohol marker pen

Teddy Clip and Miami Clip

Particular styles of Poodle clip. The Teddy Clip is an all-round length, giving a nice uniform shape. The Miami Clip is short around the muzzle and body, but leaving a long top-knot and long fur length on the legs and tail-end

Tops (roving US)

Core wool (batts US) that has undergone a further industrial process. The fleece, having been washed and carded, is then combed and stretched to straighten the fibres into what looks like 'combed hair,' and is processed into long single lengths

SUPPLIERS

World of Wool
www.worldofwool.co.uk

Adelaide Walker
www.adelaidewalker.co.uk

Felt Alive
www.feltalive.com

Felt Box (The)
wwwthefeltbox.co.uk

Heidifeathers
www.heidifeathers.com

Makerss (The)
www.themakerss.co.uk

Mum's Makery
www.mumsmakery.co.uk

Sarafina Fibre Art
www.sarafinafibreart.com

Wizpick
www.wizpick.com

For anyone who would like to link up with other like-minded needle felters of dogs, I run a very active Facebook group *Needle Felted DOGS*, on which you can show your work, ask questions about the subject, and share experiences. Existing members are friendly and helpful folk from around the world: from raw beginner to the most advanced felters, all are welcome.

Find me here –
www.chicktincreations.com
https://www.instagram.com/chicktincreations/
https://www.facebook.com/ChicktinCreations

When, in late 2018, World of Wool approached me to design some needle felting kits, I couldn't have been happier. Since then, I have written a kit every month, covering a wide range of animals.

All of the materials required are included in the kits, together with a detailed, step-by-step, photographic instructional booklet, and each teaches something new. The kits are extremely popular, and sell all around the world.